really easy piano

40 ADELE SONGS

ISBN: 978-1-70516-061-9

For all works contained herein:
Unauthorized copying, arranging, adapting, recording, internet posting, public performance,
or other distribution of the music in this publication is an infringement of copyright.
Infringers are liable under the law.

Visit Hal Leonard Online at
www.halleonard.com

Contact us:
Hal Leonard
7777 West Bluemound Road
Milwaukee, WI 53213
Email: info@halleonard.com

In Europe, contact:
Hal Leonard Europe Limited
42 Wigmore Street
Marylebone, London, W1U 2RY
Email: info@halleonardeurope.com

In Australia, contact:
Hal Leonard Australia Pty. Ltd.
4 Lentara Court
Cheltenham, Victoria, 3192 Australia
Email: info@halleonard.com.au

40 ADELE SONGS

All I Ask

Words and Music by Adele Adkins, Bruno Mars, Chris Brown and Philip Lawrence

In contrast to her first two efforts, *25* has been described by Adele as a "make-up record", and this song sums that up perfectly. She stated that she included the line "it matters how this ends" because, for her and her friends, how something ends is the most important thing because that's what sticks in your memory.

Hints & Tips: Make the most of the dynamic contrasts in this, playing
with as much feeling as you can, especially in the chorus (from bar 33).

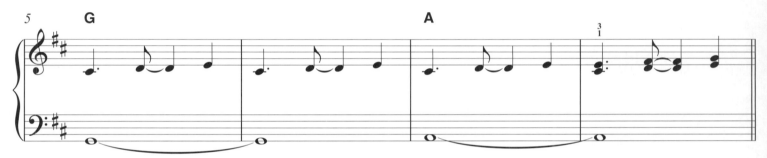

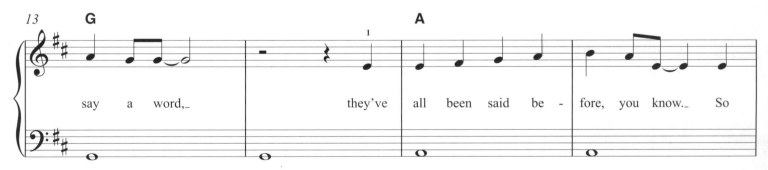

Copyright © 2015 MELTED STONE PUBLISHING LTD., BMG ONYX SONGS, MARS FORCE MUSIC, WC MUSIC CORP.,
WESTSIDE INDEPENDENT MUSIC PUBLISHING LLC, LATE 80'S MUSIC, WARNER GEO MET RIC MUSIC and ZZR MUSIC LLC
All Rights for MELTED STONE PUBLISHING LTD. in the U.S. and Canada Administered by UNIVERSAL - POLYGRAM INTERNATIONAL TUNES, INC.
All Rights for BMG ONYX SONGS and MARS FORCE MUSIC Administered by BMG RIGHTS MANAGEMENT (US) LLC
All Rights for LATE 80'S MUSIC Administered by WESTSIDE INDEPENDENT MUSIC PUBLISHING LLC
All Rights for ZZR MUSIC LLC Administered by WARNER GEO MET RIC MUSIC
All Rights Reserved   Used by Permission

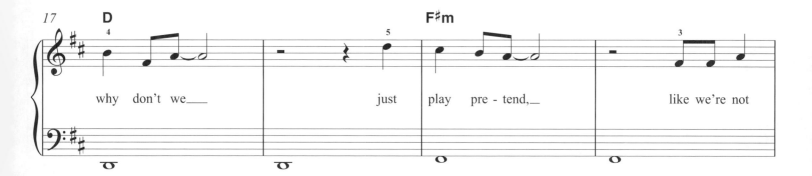

why don't we___ just play pre - tend,___ like we're not

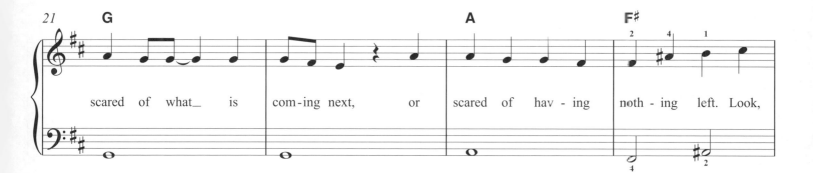

scared of what___ is com-ing next, or scared of hav - ing noth - ing left. Look,

don't get me wrong, I know there is no to - mor -

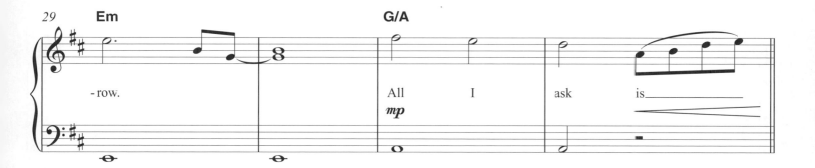

- row. All I ask is___

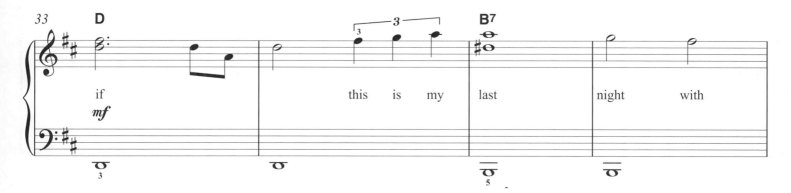

if this is my last night with

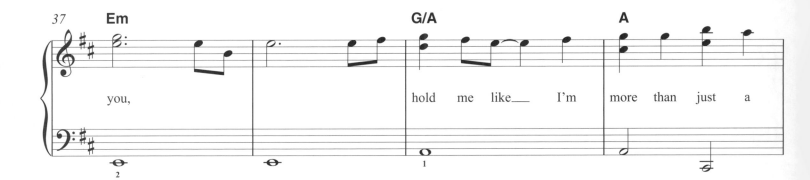

you,   hold me like___ I'm   more than just a

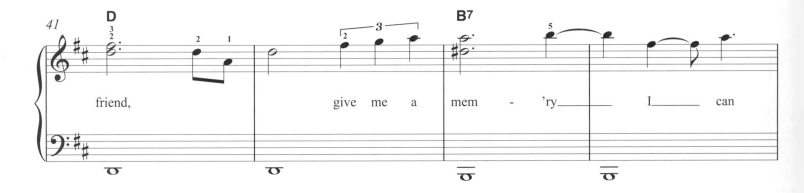

friend,   give me a mem - 'ry___ I___ can

use.   Take me by___ the   hand   while we

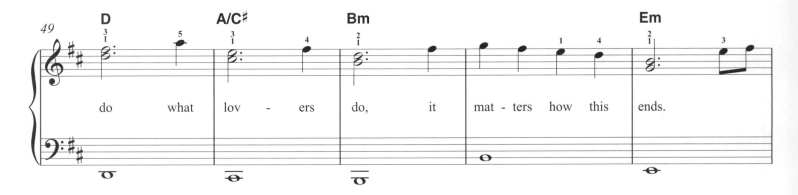

do   what lov - ers   do,   it   mat - ters how this   ends.

'Cause what if I nev - er love   a - gain?

Best for Last

Words and Music by Adele Adkins

This song features alongside 'Hometown Glory' on Adele's debut release, a limited edition 7" vinyl single released in October 2007 on the Pacemaker Recordings label. It failed to chart initially but was re-released the following year with a cover of the Etta James song 'Fool That I Am' replacing 'Best for Last'.

Hints & Tips: Although the introduction is marked freely, make sure you keep a sense of rhythm in the right hand or the feeling of the piece will be lost.

Copyright © 2008 MELTED STONE PUBLISHING LTD.
All Rights in the U.S. and Canada Administered by UNIVERSAL - POLYGRAM INTERNATIONAL TUNES, INC.
All Rights Reserved   Used by Permission

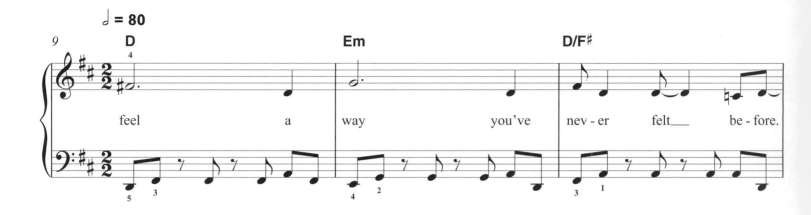

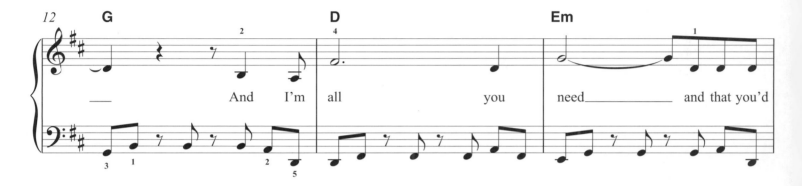

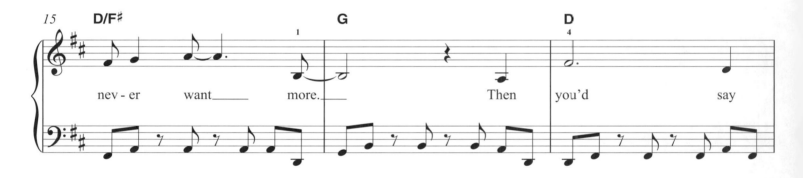

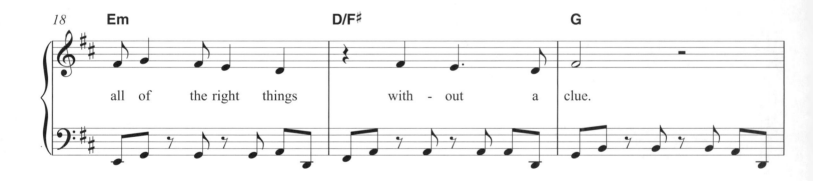

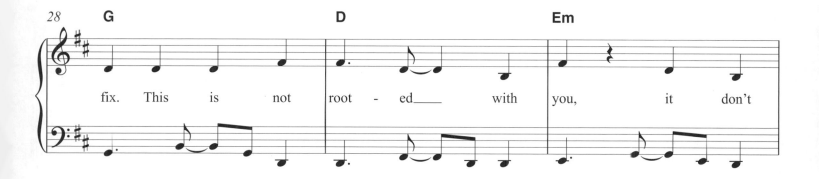

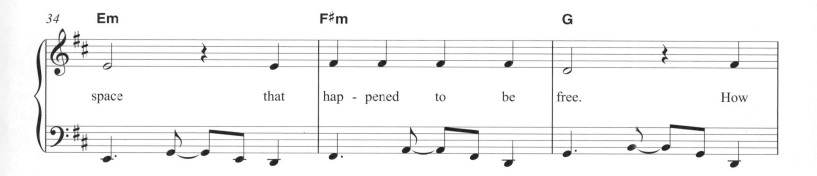

Can I Get It

Words and Music by Adele Adkins, Shellback and Max Martin

From her 2021 album, *30*, 'Can I Get It' is about Adele longing for a real relationship instead of just casual dating, after divorcing her husband Simon Konecki. The song was written with Max Martin and his regular collaborator, Shellback. Martin has co-written many hit songs including Kelly Clarkson's 'Since U Been Gone', Katy Perry's 'I Kissed a Girl' and Taylor Swift's 'Shake It Off' and holds third place for the most number one singles on the Billboard Hot 100 chart, behind Paul McCartney and John Lennon!

Hints & Tips: This song has a driving pulse, lead mainly by the left hand. Try a slower tempo at first, until you're comfortable with the left-hand motif in the verse.

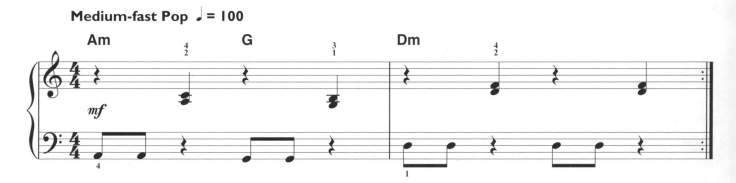

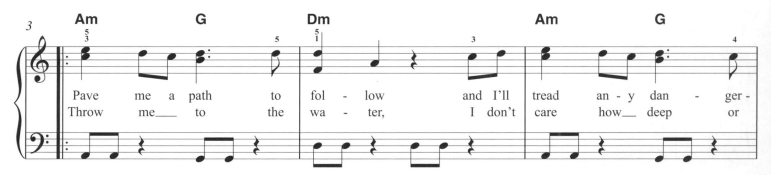

Copyright © 2021 MELTED STONE PUBLISHING LTD. and MXM
All Rights for MELTED STONE PUBLISHING LTD. in the U.S. and Canada Administered by UNIVERSAL - POLYGRAM INTERNATIONAL TUNES, INC.
All Rights for MXM Administered Worldwide by KOBALT SONGS MUSIC PUBLISHING
All Rights Reserved   Used by Permission

I have prom-ised I___ will love you till___ the end of time,_____

through it all, the good,_ the bad, the ug - ly, and di - vine._____

I will be the mel - o - dy, the rhy - thm, and your rhyme._____

all I want is for__ you to be mine._____ So can I get it right

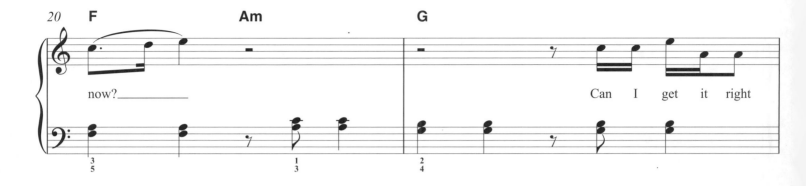

now?

Can I get it right

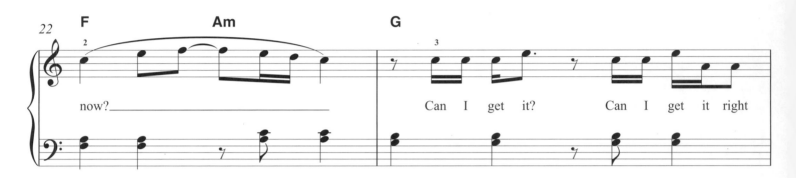

now?

Can I get it?   Can I get it right

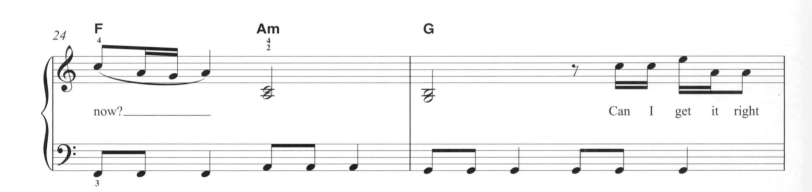

now?

Can I get it right

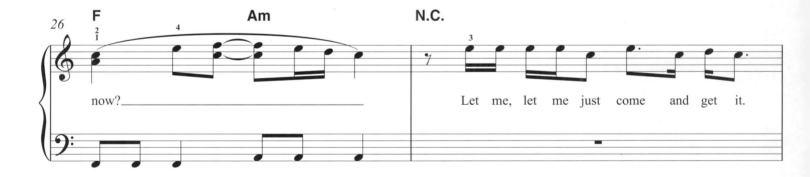

now?

Let me, let me just come and get it.

Can I get it?

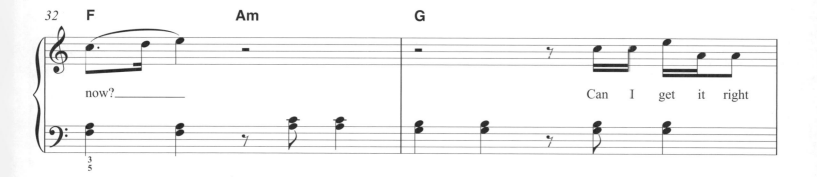

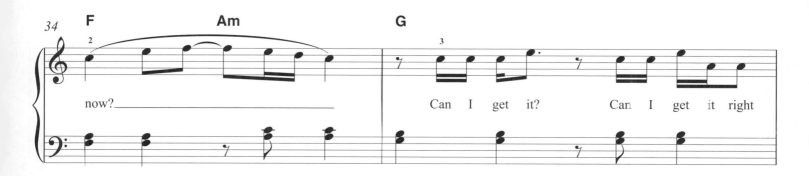

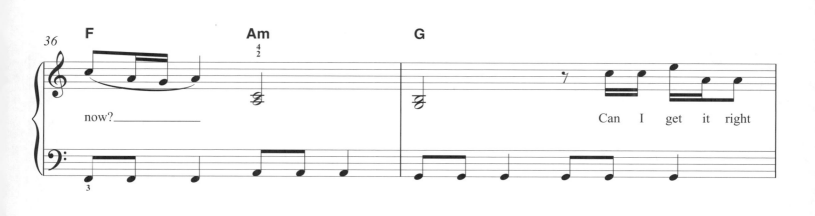

Chasing Pavements

Words and Music by Adele Adkins and Francis Eg White

Adele was awarded the 2009 Grammy Award for Best Female Pop Vocal Performance for her recording of this mellow, sensuous slice of old-school soul. A hymn to lost love and regret, 'Chasing Pavements' was written after an argument she had with a boyfriend in a London bar, after which she stormed out and began running down Oxford Street.

Hints & Tips: Practise the winding left-hand part in the first seven bars of this piece separately, paying careful attention to the fingering, before putting it together with the right hand.

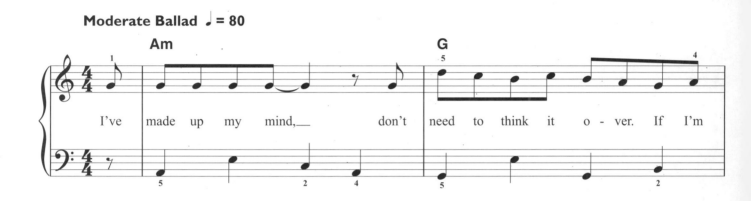

Copyright © 2008 MELTED STONE PUBLISHING LTD. and UNIVERSAL MUSIC PUBLISHING LTD.
All Rights for MELTED STONE PUBLISHING LTD. in the U.S. and Canada Administered by UNIVERSAL - POLYGRAM INTERNATIONAL TUNES, INC.
All Rights for UNIVERSAL MUSIC PUBLISHING LTD. in the U.S. and Canada Controlled and Administered by UNIVERSAL - POLYGRAM INTERNATIONAL PUBLISHING, INC.
All Rights Reserved   Used by Permission

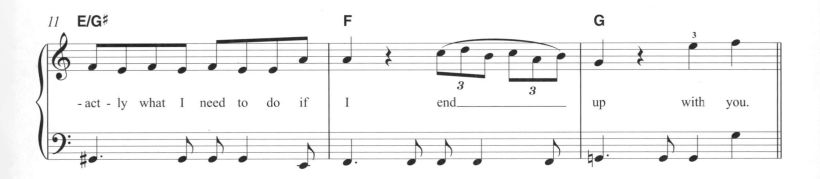

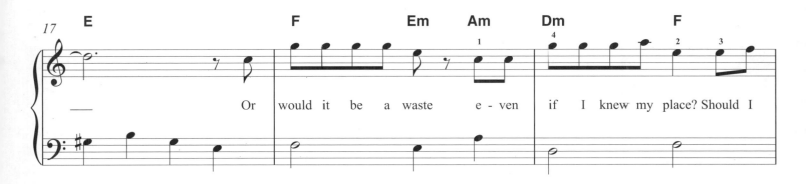

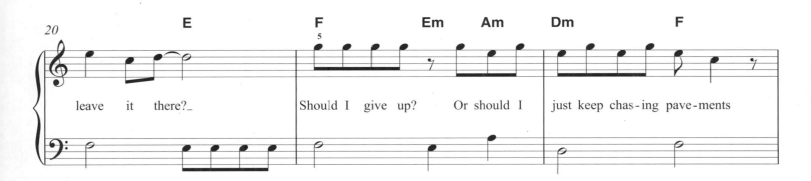

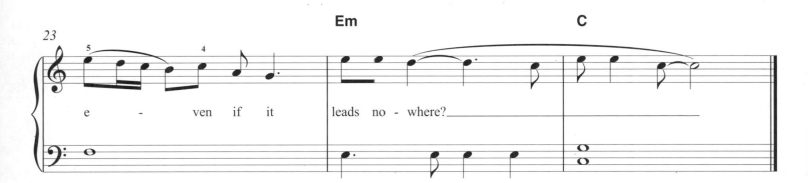

Cold Shoulder

Words and Music by Adele Adkins and Sacha Skarbek

The third single released from her first album and the only track on the album produced by Mark Ronson, this song peaked at No. 18 in the UK Singles Chart. Adele rose in prominence in America following a performance of both 'Cold Shoulder' and 'Chasing Pavements' on Saturday Night Live in October 2008.

Hints & Tips: The right hand changes position quite a lot, so make sure you look through the fingering so you know when to move.

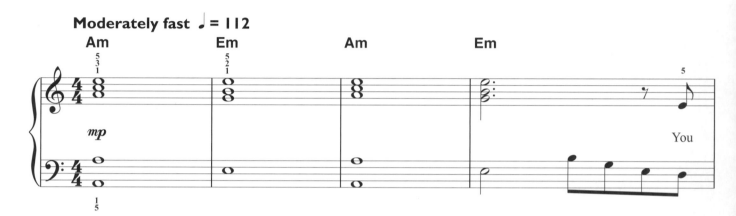

Copyright © 2008 MELTED STONE PUBLISHING LTD. and UNIVERSAL MUSIC PUBLISHING LTD.
All Rights in the U.S. and Canada Administered by UNIVERSAL - POLYGRAM INTERNATIONAL TUNES, INC.
All Rights Reserved   Used by Permission

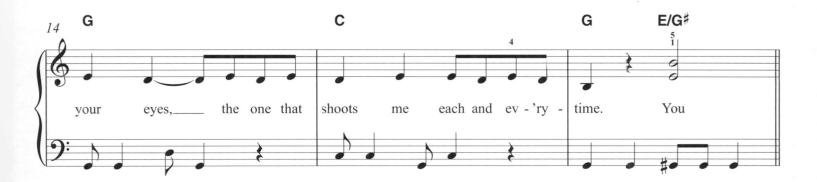

your eyes,_____ the one that shoots me each and ev-'ry - time. You

grace me with your cold shoul - der_____ when-ev - er you look at me and wish I was

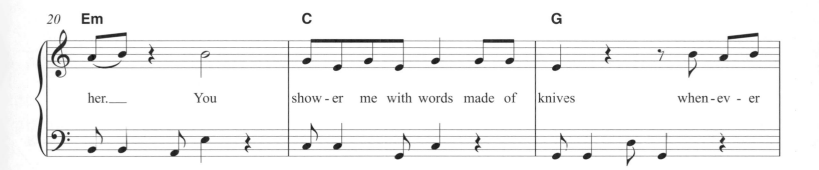

her._____ You show - er me with words made of knives when-ev - er

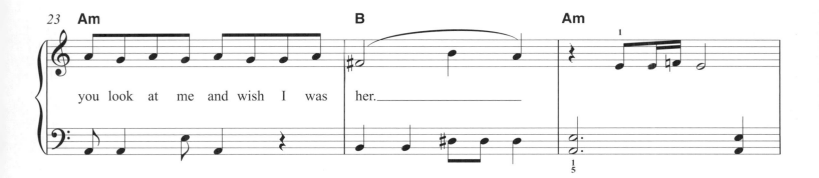

you look at me and wish I was her._____

Crazy for You

Words and Music by Adele Adkins

Adele once admitted that she finds it more difficult to write songs when she is in love, and this ballad is a rare example of a positive declaration of affection. Both *19* and *21* were composed in the wake of the end of relationships and themes of heartbreak and bitterness dominate throughout.

Hints & Tips: There are quite a few accidentals in bars 29—31 in both the left and right hand. Play through this passage to familiarise yourself with the fingering.

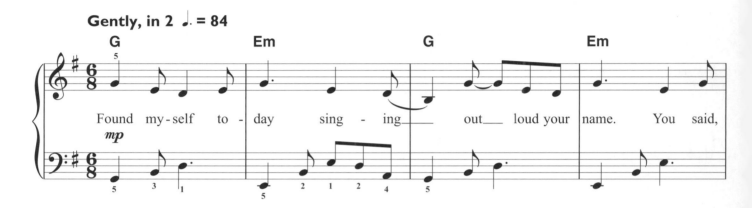

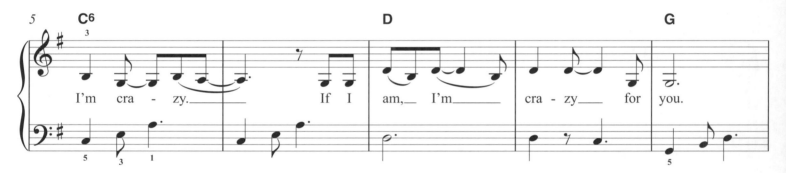

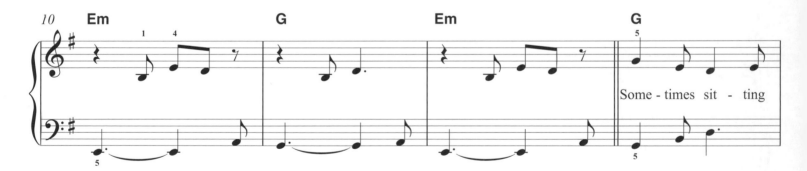

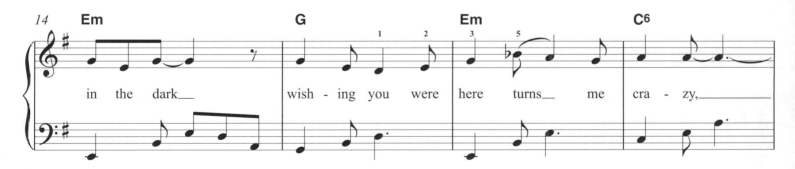

Copyright © 2008 MELTED STONE PUBLISHING LTD.
All Rights in the U.S. and Canada Administered by UNIVERSAL - POLYGRAM INTERNATIONAL TUNES, INC.
All Rights Reserved   Used by Permission

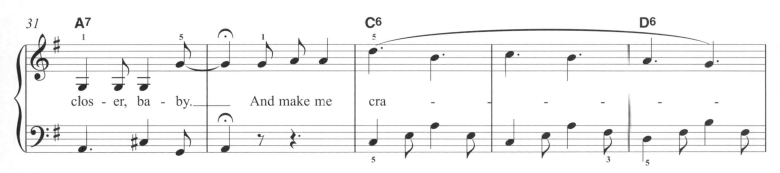

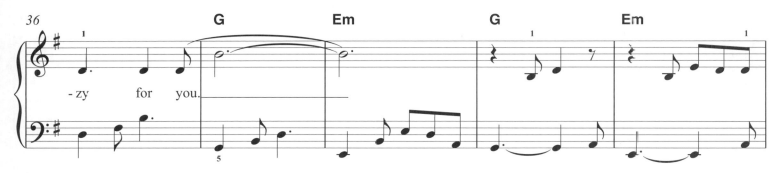

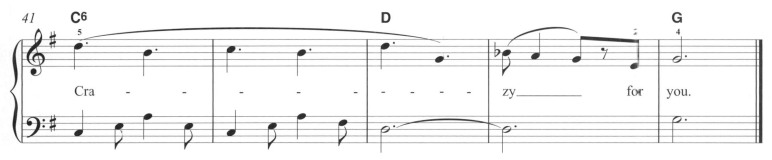

19

Daydreamer

Words and Music by Adele Adkins

This ballad, the opening track on her debut album *19*, is one of several produced by the Mercury Award-winning producer Jim Abbiss. Adele made her debut TV performance with this song in 2007 on the BBC's *Later with Jools Holland*, alongside performances by Sir Paul McCartney and Björk.

Hints & Tips: Play the left hand through first to make sure you can play it nice and evenly before joining in with the right hand. Look out for the time signature change in bars 9 and 33.

Copyright © 2008 MELTED STONE PUBLISHING LTD.
All Rights in the U.S. and Canada Administered by UNIVERSAL - POLYGRAM INTERNATIONAL TUNES, INC.
All Rights Reserved   Used by Permission

20

he could change the world with his hands be-hind his back, oh.__

24

You can find him

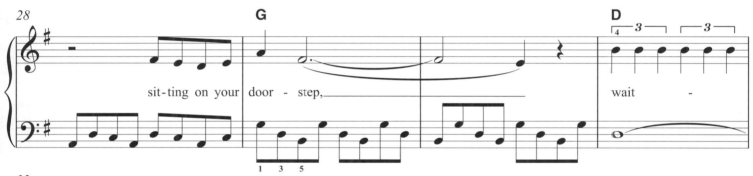

28

sit-ting on your door - step,____ wait -

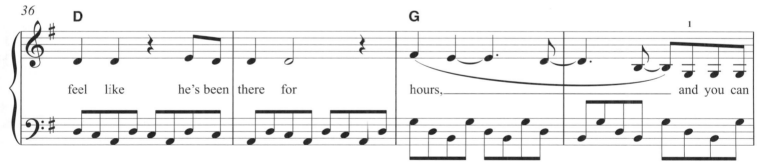

32

- ing__ for____ the sur - prise. And he will

36

feel like he's been there for hours,____ and you can

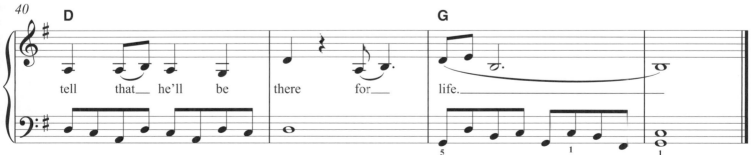

40

tell that__ he'll be there for__ life.__

Don't You Remember

Words and Music by Adele Adkins and Dan Wilson

Adele's second album *21* was released in January 2011 and debuted at the top of the UK album chart in its first week of release. This country ballad was written in an effort to compensate for the overly bitter tone of the rest of the album; in it she reminisces about the feelings of first falling in love.

Hints & Tips: Start softly, so you can build up to the chorus, making the most of the triplets.

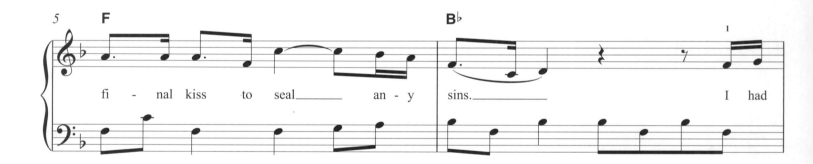

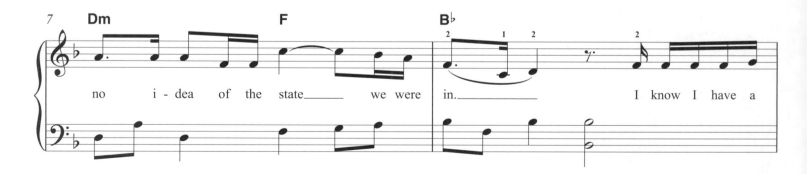

Copyright © 2010, 2011 MELTED STONE PUBLISHING LTD., BMG MONARCH and SUGAR LAKE MUSIC
All Rights for MELTED STONE PUBLISHING LTD. in the U.S. and Canada Administered by UNIVERSAL - POLYGRAM INTERNATIONAL TUNES, INC.
All Rights for BMG MONARCH and SUGAR LAKE MUSIC Administered by BMG RIGHTS MANAGEMENT (US) LLC
All Rights Reserved   Used by Permission

fick-le heart   and a bit-ter-ness.   And a wond'ring eye   and a heav-i-ness in my__ head.

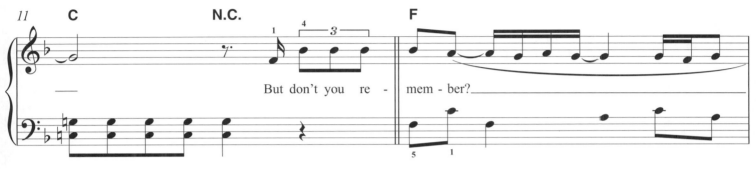

__   But don't you re - mem - ber?_____

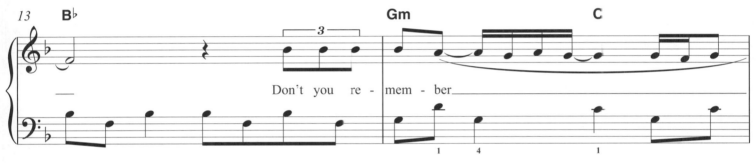

__   Don't you re - mem - ber_____

__   the rea - son you loved me_____   be -

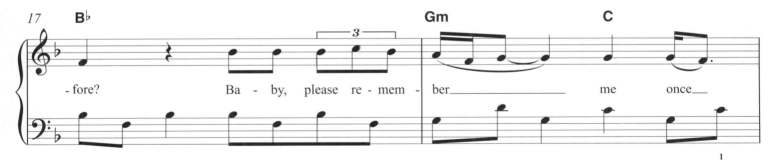

- fore?   Ba - by, please re - mem - ber_____ me   once__

more.   When   will   I   see you____   a - gain?_____

Easy on Me

Words and Music by Adele Adkins and Greg Kurstin

This track is Adele's lead single from her fourth studio album, *30*, released in 2021. It is also the singer's third No. 1, after previous chart toppers 'Someone Like You' and 'Hello'. 'Easy on Me' was written after the breakup of her marriage, with Adele asking for understanding from her ex-husband, Simon Konecki, and their son, Angelo. After writing this song, the British songstress had a 6-month song writing hiatus before continuing to pen tracks for this album.

Hints & Tips: This is a gentle ballad; keep it steady and don't play too loud.
Feel free to remove the lower right-hand notes if they're too much of a stretch.

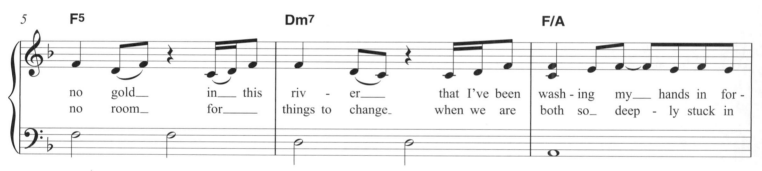

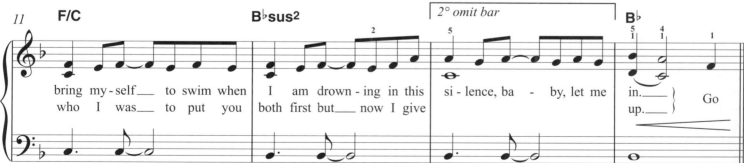

Copyright © 2021 MELTED STONE PUBLISHING LTD., EMI APRIL MUSIC INC. and KURSTIN MUSIC
All Rights for MELTED STONE PUBLISHING LTD. in the U.S. and Canada Administered by UNIVERSAL - POLYGRAM INTERNATIONAL TUNES, INC.
All Rights for EMI APRIL MUSIC INC. and KURSTIN MUSIC Administered by SONY MUSIC PUBLISHING (US) LLC, 424 Church Street, Suite 1200, Nashville, TN 37219
All Rights Reserved   Used by Permission

ea - - - sy on me, ba - by, I was still a child, did-n't

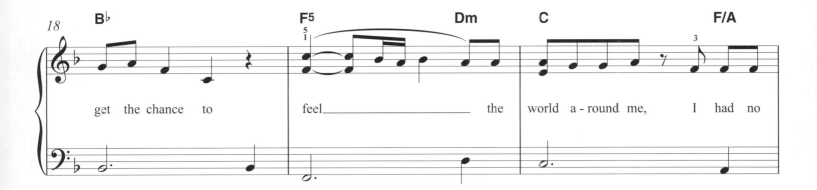

get the chance to feel_____ the world a - round me, I had no

1.

time to choose_ what I chose to do, so go ea - sy on me.

2.

ea - sy _____ on me.

First Love

Words and Music by Adele Adkins

Adele was announced as the first recipient of the BRIT Awards Critics' Choice Award in December 2007.
The award is open to artists set to release their debut album the following year and is chosen by a panel
of experts and critics. It has since been won by Florence + The Machine, Ellie Goulding and Jessie J.

Hints & Tips: Make sure the left hand is even and consistent.
Check through the right-hand fingering, as the melody has a few stretches.

Copyright © 2008 MELTED STONE PUBLISHING LTD.
All Rights in the U.S. and Canada Administered by UNIVERSAL - POLYGRAM INTERNATIONAL TUNES, INC.
All Rights Reserved   Used by Permission

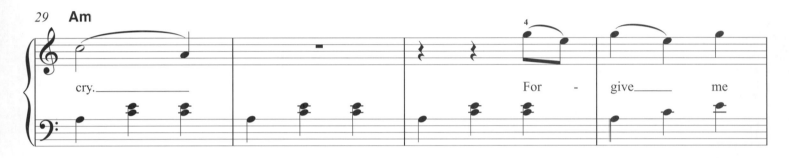

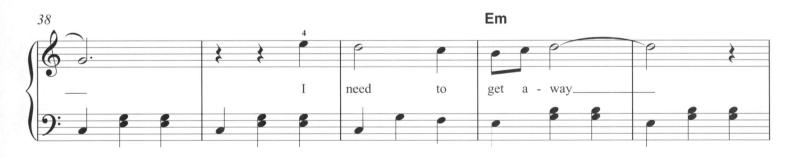

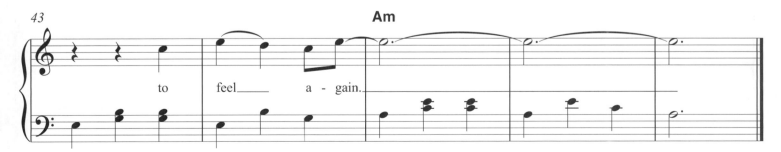

He Won't Go

Words and Music by Adele Adkins and Paul Epworth

A graduate of the BRIT School for Performing Arts & Technology and classmate of Leona Lewis and Jessie J, Adele wrote this lilting R'n'B track about two of her close friends. When the couple became an 'item', she was inspired by the strength of their relationship in the face of adversity.

Hints & Tips: The melody is in the left hand, so make sure you keep the right hand light so it comes through. Play the left hand on its own until you're sure of the rhythm and the fingering.

Copyright © 2010, 2011 MELTED STONE PUBLISHING LTD. and EMI MUSIC PUBLISHING LTD.
All Rights for MELTED STONE PUBLISHING LTD. in the U.S. and Canada Administered by UNIVERSAL - POLYGRAM INTERNATIONAL TUNES, INC.
All Rights for EMI MUSIC PUBLISHING LTD. Administered by SONY MUSIC PUBLISHING (US) LLC, 424 Church Street, Suite 1200, Nashville, TN 37219
All Rights Reserved   Used by Permission

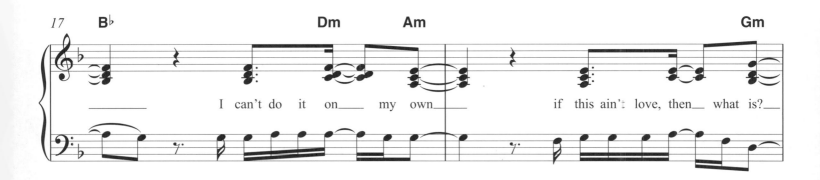

I can't do it on___ my own___ if this ain't love, then___ what is?___

I'm will-ing to take___ the risk. I won't___ go.___

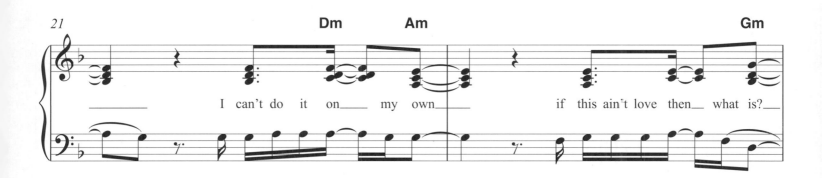

I can't do it on___ my own___ if this ain't love then___ what is?___

I'm will-ing to take___ the risk.___

rall.

Hometown Glory

Words and Music by Adele Adkins

Following critical acclaim for this evocative portrait of her fondest memories of London, at 19 years old, Adele was already tipped for future success by topping the BBC's Sound of 2008 poll. The song has gone on to be included in many TV shows, including *Skins*, *Grey's Anatomy* and *One Tree Hill*.

Hints & Tips: The leaps in the left hand might be too wide for your hand to span. If this is the case, gently 'rock' between the two, playing each note for as near to its full length as you can.

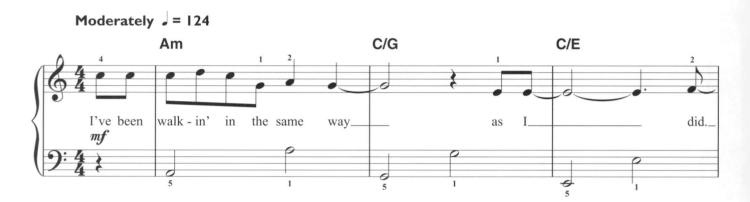

I've been walk-in' in the same way___ as I_____ did._

___ And miss-ing out the cracks in the pave - ment and tut-tin' my heel and strut-tin' my

feet. "Is there an-y-thing I can do for you,_ dear? Is there__ an-y-one I could

call?" "No and thank you, please, mad - am. I ain't lost_ just wan-

Copyright © 2008 MELTED STONE PUBLISHING LTD.
All Rights in the U.S. and Canada Administered by UNIVERSAL - POLYGRAM INTERNATIONAL TUNES, INC.
All Rights Reserved   Used by Permission

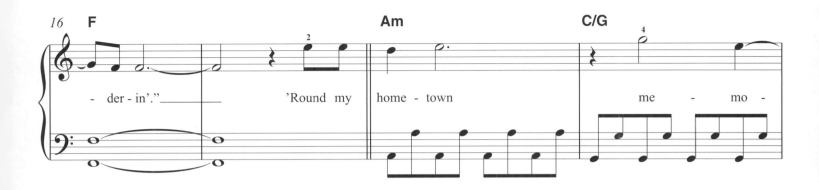

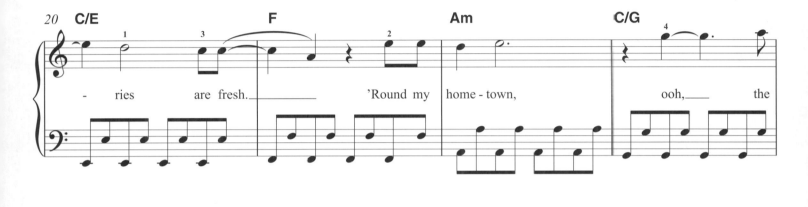

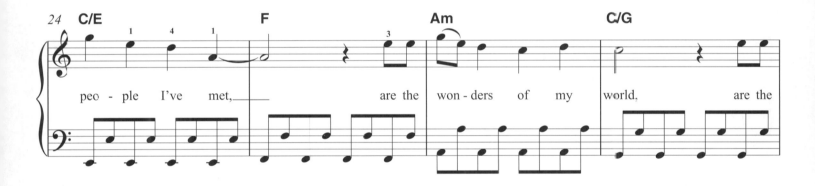

Hello

Words and Music by Adele Adkins and Greg Kurstin

As speculation about Adele's new music in 2015 reached its peak, a cryptic advert appeared on UK TV which featured the first verse of this song. Adele had finally said "Hello" again to her fans after a three-year break from music, and the song was unveiled as the first single from her album *25*. The emotional ballad marked a stunning return for the 27 year-old, debuting at No. 1 in the UK Charts in October 2015.

Hints & Tips: Count the rhythms of all the tied notes carefully before you begin. This rhythm is repeated throughout.

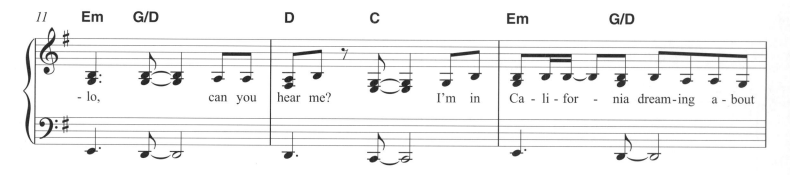

Copyright © 2015 MELTED STONE PUBLISHING LTD., EMI APRIL MUSIC INC. and KURSTIN MUSIC
All Rights for MELTED STONE PUBLISHING LTD. in the U.S. and Canada Administered by UNIVERSAL - POLYGRAM INTERNATIONAL TUNES, INC.
All Rights for EMI APRIL MUSIC INC. and KURSTIN MUSIC Administered by SONY MUSIC PUBLISHING (US) LLC, 424 Church Street, Suite 1200, Nashville, TN 37219
All Rights Reserved   Used by Permission

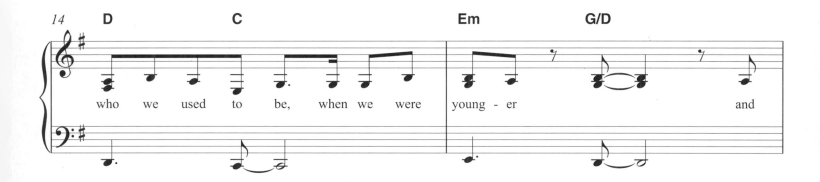

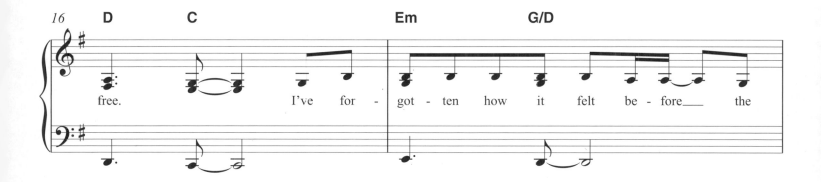

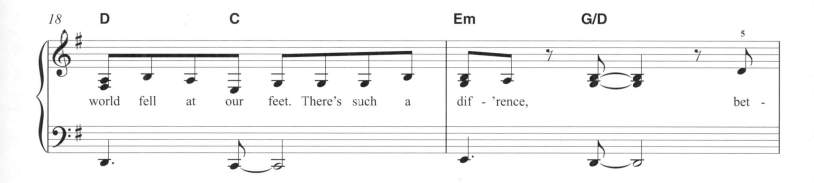

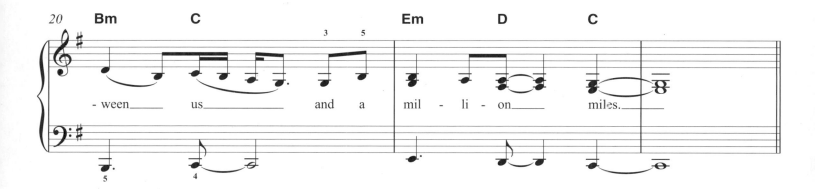

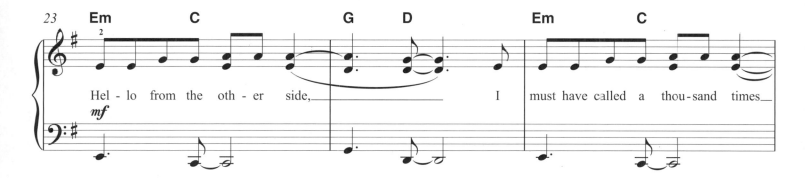

to tell you___ I'm sor - ry for ev -'ry - thing that I've done,___ but when I call___

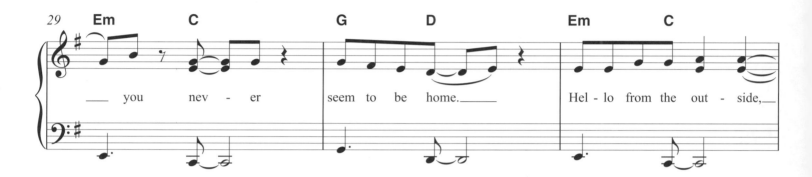

___ you nev - er seem to be home._____ Hel - lo from the out - side,___

_____ at least I can say that I've tried_____ to tell you___

___ I'm sor - ry for break - ing your heart,___ but it don't mat - ter, it clear - ly does - n't

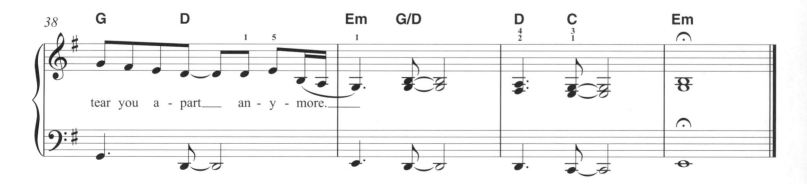

tear you a - part___ an - y - more.___

Hold On

Words and Music by Adele Adkins and Dean Josiah Cover

This gospel-inspired track features Adele's friends as her backing vocalists. Adele wanted to include her real-life support network in this track singing 'just hold on' because this is what her friends would actually say to her during her divorce. The song features in an Amazon Christmas holiday advert where a woman buys a surprise gift for her curious younger neighbour out of kindness. It debuted live in November 2021 as part of the CBS primetime special 'Adele: One Night Only', where Adele was also interviewed by Oprah Winfrey.

Hints & Tips: This is a slow song with long, held chords in the left hand. The right hand should sound conversational in the verse (from bar 17), so the rhythm can be approximate. Keep it gentle overall, apart from the last page where it builds to a climax.

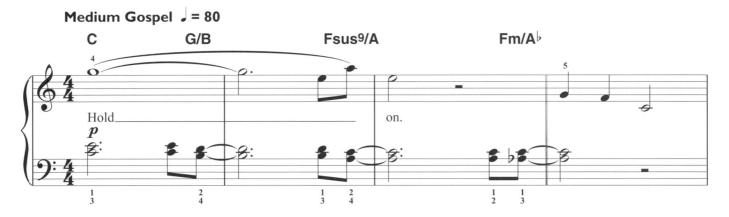

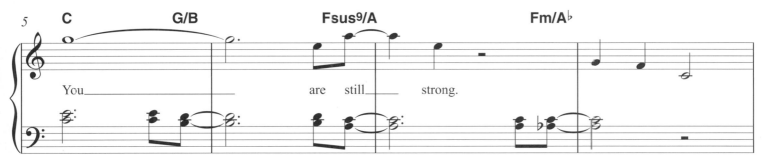

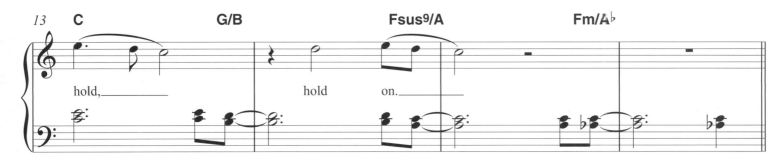

Copyright © 2021 MELTED STONE PUBLISHING LTD. and DEAN JOSIAH COVER PUBLISHING DESIGNEE
All Rights for MELTED STONE PUBLISHING LTD. in the U.S. and Canada Administered by UNIVERSAL - POLYGRAM INTERNATIONAL TUNES, INC.
All Rights Reserved   Used by Permission

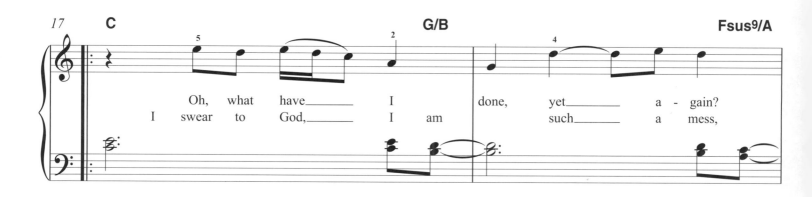

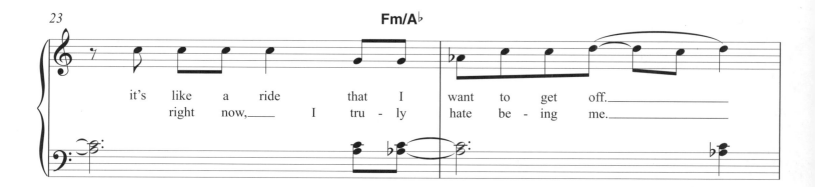

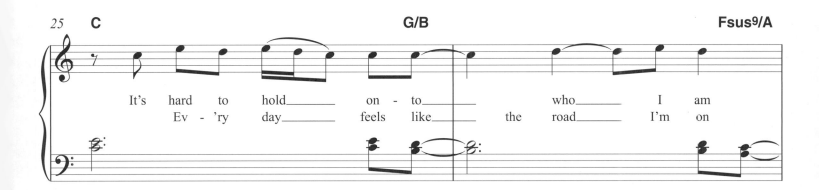

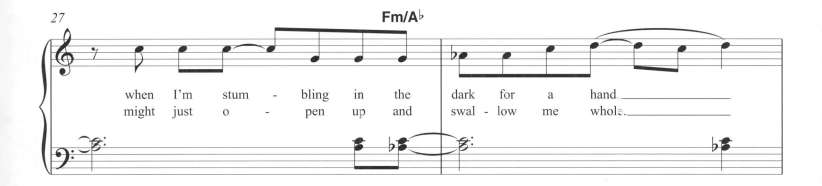

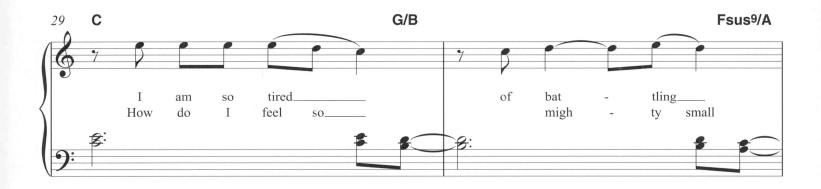

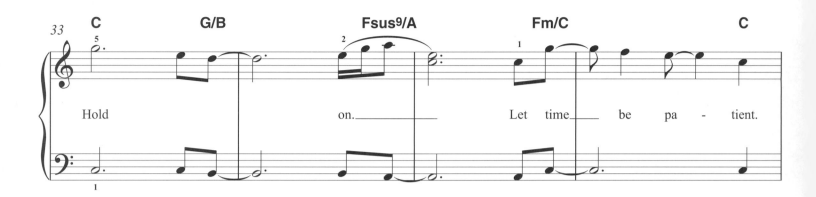

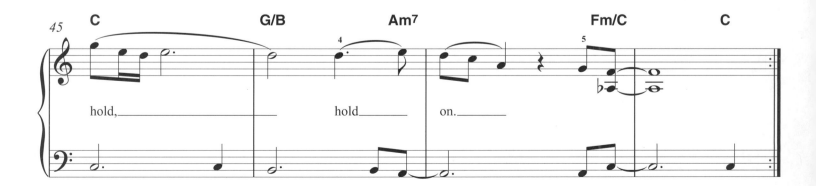

Love_____ will soon come,_____ ba - by,   if you

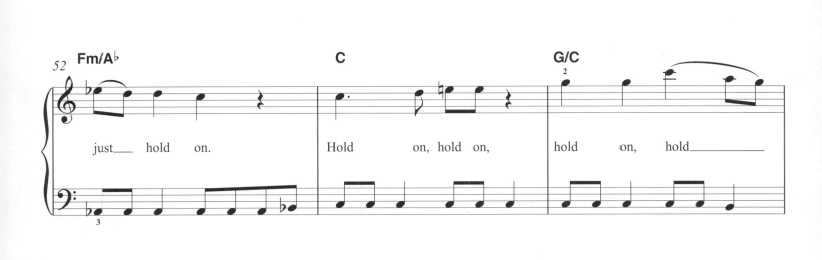

just___ hold   on.   Hold   on, hold on,   hold   on,   hold_____

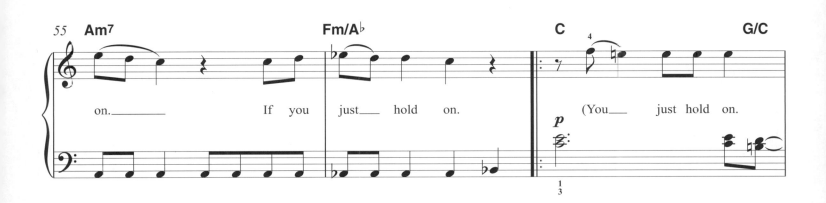

on._____   If you just___ hold   on.   (You___   just hold on.

You___   just hold on.   You___   just hold on.   Just hold on,   just hold on.)

I Miss You

Words and Music by Adele Adkins and Paul Epworth

'I Miss You' was written over a night when Adele couldn't sleep, finishing it with Paul Epworth later on. Epworth co-wrote Adele's 2010 smash hit, 'Rolling in the Deep' and her Bond song for the 2012 film, *Skyfall*, so the pair have undeniable collaboration chemistry! Speaking of this song from her 2015 album, *25*, Adele says 'it's about intimacy on every level' in an interview with i-D Magazine, with the album itself described as a 'make-up record', detailing 'nostalgia' and 'melancholia about the passage of time'.

Hints & Tips: Enjoy the dark nature of this song. The left hand has the same dotted rhythm throughout, but the right hand has a lot more variety. Just miss out the intro if you're not comfortable playing the chords.

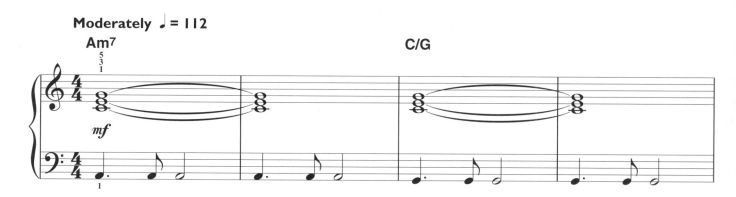

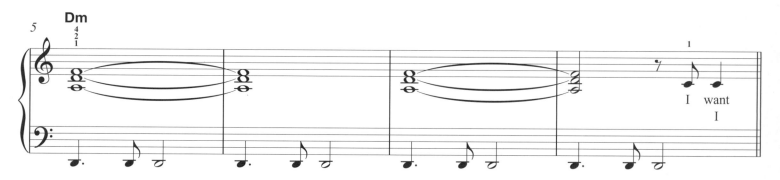

Copyright © 2015 MELTED STONE PUBLISHING LTD. and EMI MUSIC PUBLISHING LTD.
All Rights for MELTED STONE PUBLISHING LTD. in the U.S. and Canada Administered by UNIVERSAL - POLYGRAM INTERNATIONAL TUNES, INC.
All Rights for EMI MUSIC PUBLISHING LTD. Administered by SONY MUSIC PUBLISHING (US) LLC, 424 Church Street, Suite 1200, Nashville, TN 37219
All Rights Reserved   Used by Permission

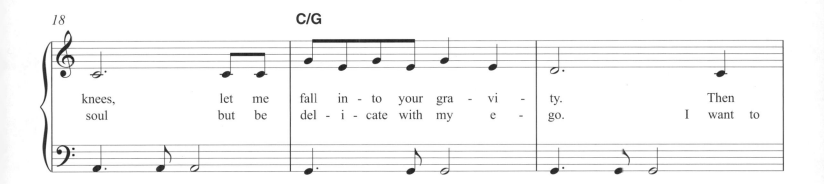

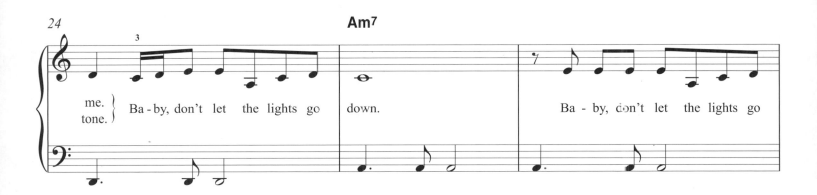

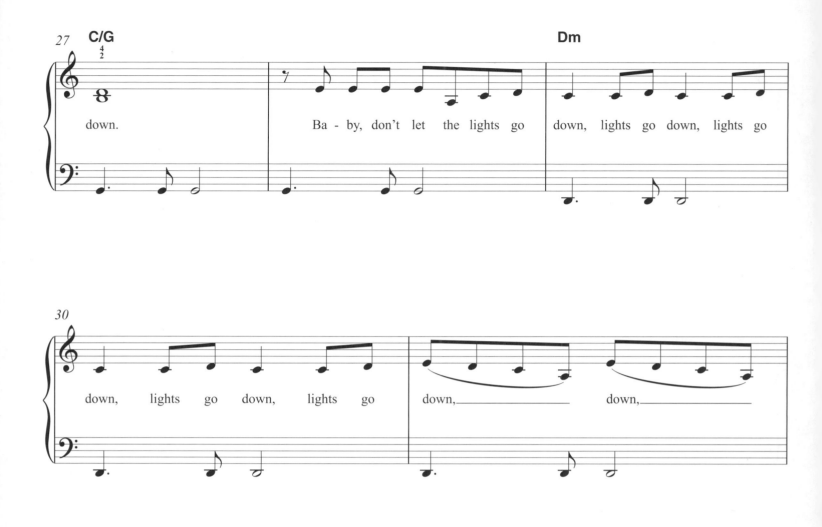

hold me tight,_____ don't let go,_____ ba - by, give me light._____ I

miss you when the lights go out, it il - lu - - - mi - nates all

of my doubts._____ Pull me in,_____ hold me tight,_____

don't let go,_____ ba - by, give me light._____

I Drink Wine

Words and Music by Adele Adkins and Greg Kurstin

Greg Kurstin co-wrote this track with Adele, whom she started working with on her previous album, *25*. The pair collaborated on almost half of the tracks on *30*, the album that 'I Drink Wine' appears on. It was originally 15 minutes long and Adele titled it in jest, before she was asked to cut it down for radio play and decided to keep the song title. It is a swung, jazz-inspired track from the songstress and shows her evolution into new styles and influences for this 2021 record.

Hints & Tips: Take time to get into the gentle 'swing' groove in this song. The right hand has a two-octave range, so you may need to spend time practising it on its own to get the fingering right.

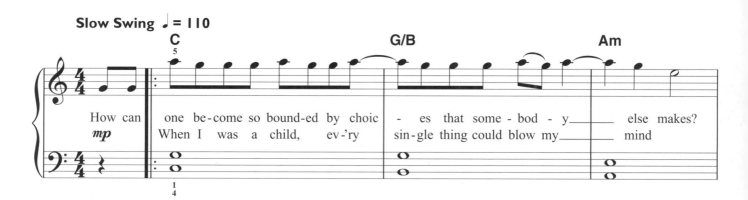

Copyright © 2021 MELTED STONE PUBLISHING LTD., EMI APRIL MUSIC INC. and KURSTIN MUSIC
All Rights for MELTED STONE PUBLISHING LTD. in the U.S. and Canada Administered by UNIVERSAL - POLYGRAM INTERNATIONAL TUNES, INC.
All Rights for EMI APRIL MUSIC INC. and KURSTIN MUSIC Administered by SONY MUSIC PUBLISHING (US) LLC, 424 Church Street, Suite 1200, Nashville, TN 37219
All Rights Reserved   Used by Permission

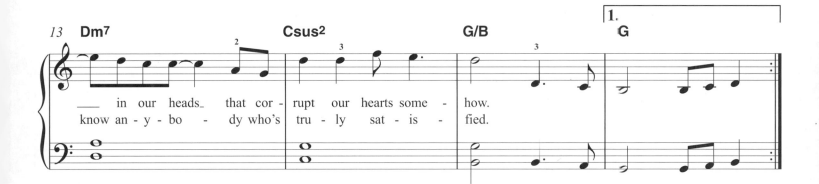

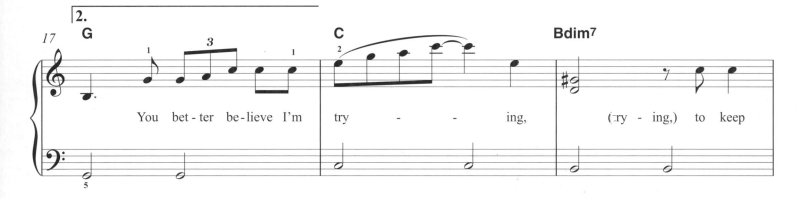

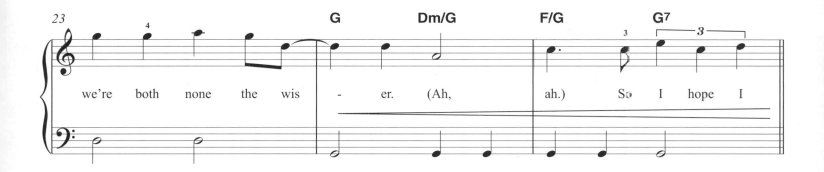

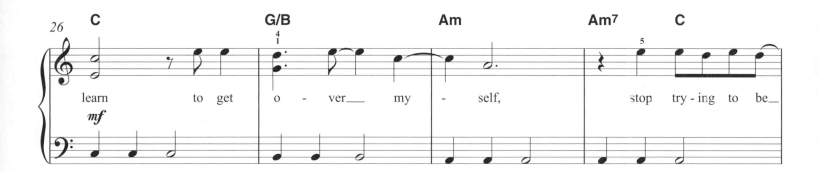

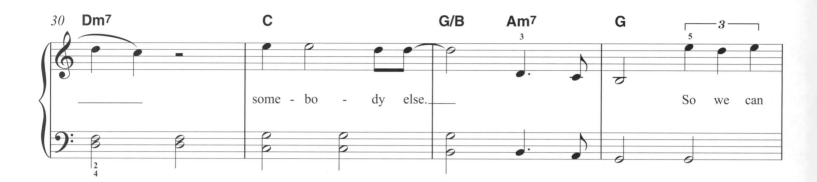

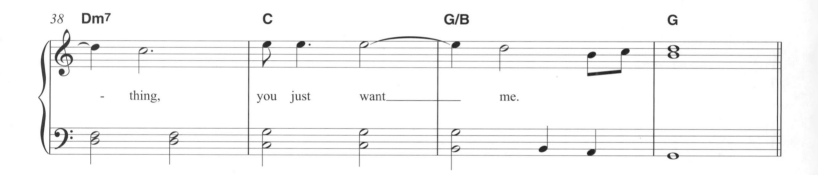

Love Is a Game

Words and Music by Adele Adkins and Dean Josiah Cover

This is the final track on the *30* album from 2021, where Adele sings about the heartache, trials and tribulations of love but how she's willing and ready to go through it all again. 'Love Is a Game' has influences of soul and motown, likely as a result of Adele's collaboration with producer, Inflo, who is well known for a production infused with the warmth of 70's soul. The London-bred creative won 'Producer of the Year' at the 2022 Brit Awards after his work with Adele, Michael Kiwanuka and Little Simz and was the first black producer to do so.

Hints & Tips: Take a moment to understand the structure of the verse, with its two repeats and 1st and 2nd time bars. Keep this one slow; it should sound very relaxed and gentle in the verse, but build up to a much louder chorus.

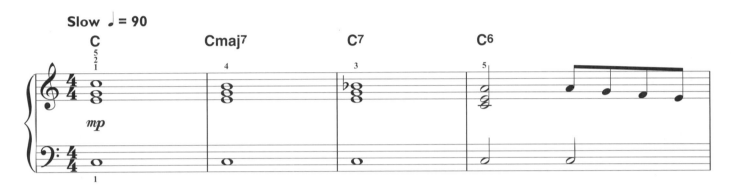

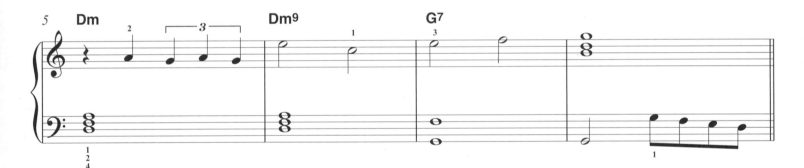

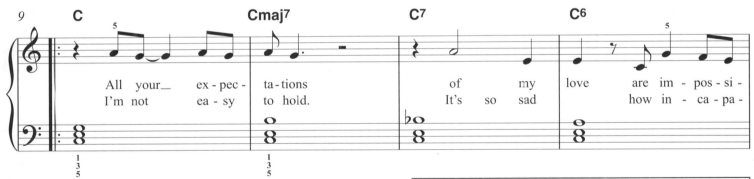

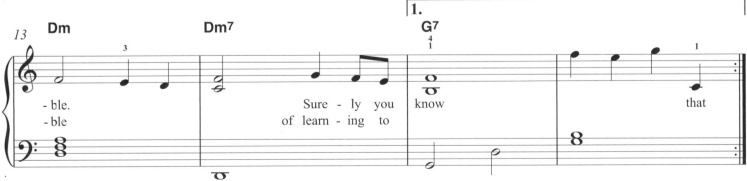

Copyright © 2021 MELTED STONE PUBLISHING LTD. and DEAN JOSIAH COVER PUBLISHING DESIGNEE
All Rights for MELTED STONE PUBLISHING LTD. in the U.S. and Canada Administered by UNIVERSAL - POLYGRAM INTERNATIONAL TUNES, INC.
All Rights Reserved   Used by Permission

grow   I   am.___   My heart__ speaks in
                         I can't__ take an-

puz - zle and codes,___   I've been   try - ing my whole life to
-oth - er de - feat,___   a next time___   would be the end - ing of

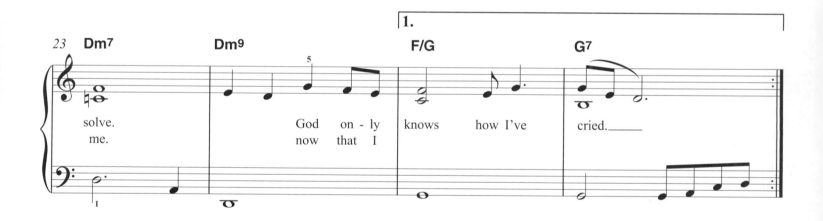

1.

solve.   God on - ly   knows   how I've   cried.___
me.   now that I

2.

see,___   ee - ee - ee - ee.   That love   is a game for

fools   to   play_____   and I ain't   fool - ing,   what a

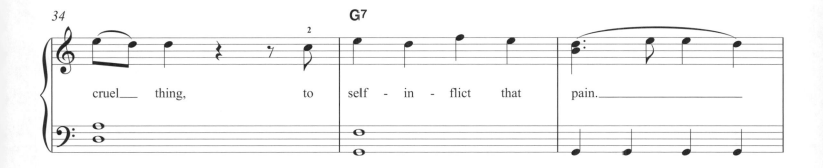

cruel___ thing,   to   self - in - flict that   pain._____

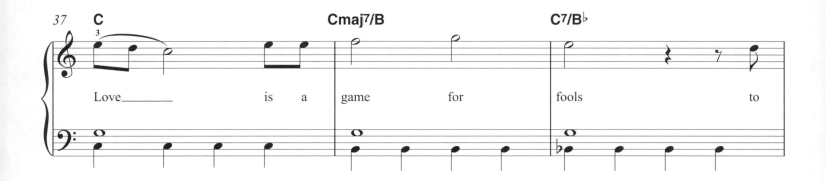

Love_____   is a   game   for   fools   to

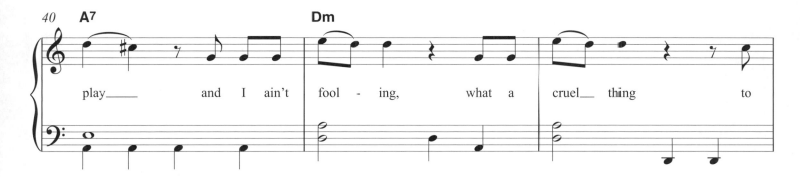

play_____   and I ain't   fool - ing,   what a   cruel___ thing   to

rall.

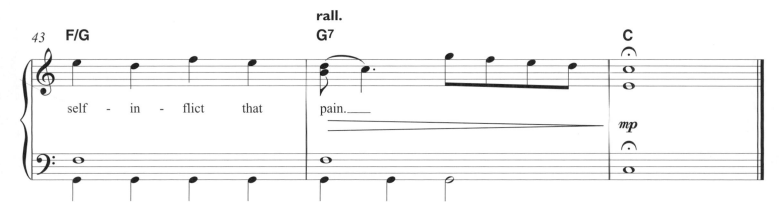

self - in - flict that   pain._____

Love in the Dark

Words and Music by Adele Adkins and Samuel Dixon

While Adele's customary lyric writing is centred around events that happen to her in relationships, 'Love in the Dark' turns this on its head somewhat with the singer talking about taking the reins and ending a relationship because the love has faded. It is the only song on her *25* album with a string section and was co-written with her bassist from the *21* album tour, Samuel Dixon, who has also worked with Jack Savoretti, Katie Melua and Sia.

Hints & Tips: You could treat the intro as optional if you find the offbeat, 'syncopated' rhythm too tricky. This is a good song for practising your left-hand triads (chords). Play the chorus loud.

Copyright © 2015 MELTED STONE PUBLISHING LTD. and BMG RIGHTS MANAGEMENT (UK) LTD.
All Rights for MELTED STONE PUBLISHING LTD. in the U.S. and Canada Administered by UNIVERSAL - POLYGRAM INTERNATIONAL TUNES, INC.
All Rights for BMG RIGHTS MANAGEMENT (UK) LTD. Administered by BMG RIGHTS MANAGEMENT (US) LLC
All Rights Reserved   Used by Permission

13 **Em**   **F**   **Am**

with   you   watch -   ing   me.   But   This   is   nev -   er
when   you   are   in   doubt.   I   don't   want   to

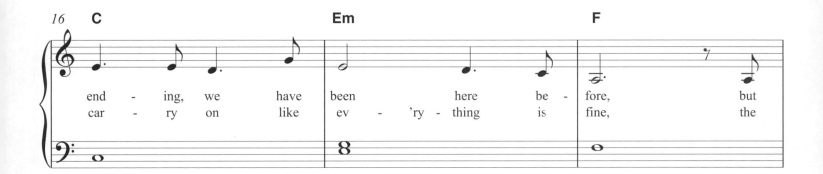

16 **C**   **Em**   **F**

end -   ing,   we   have   been   here   be -   fore,   but
car -   ry   on   like   ev -   'ry -   thing   is   fine,   the

19 **Am**   **C**   **Em**

I   can't   stay   this   time   'cause   I   don't   love   you   an -   y -
long -   er   we   ig -   nore   it   all   the   more   that   we   will

22 **F**   **Am**   **Cmaj⁷**

-more.   Please_____   stay   where   you   are_____   don't   come
fight.   Please_____   don't   fall   a -   part_____   I   can't

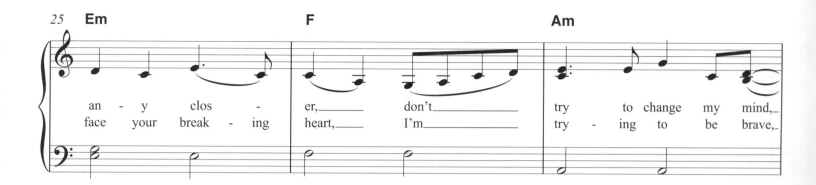

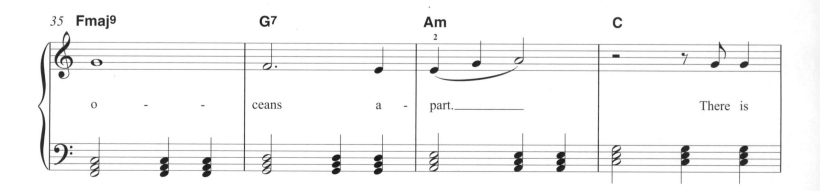

so much space be - tween____ us, ba - by, we're al - read - y de - feat -

- ed, yeah,____ ev - 'ry - thing

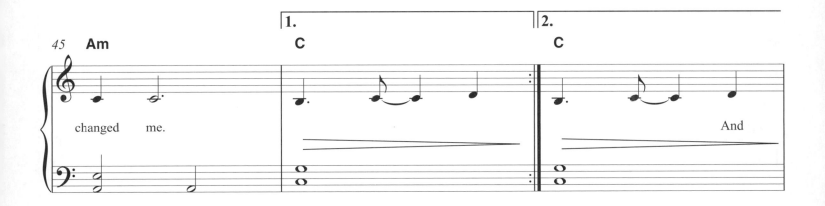

changed me.

1.

2.

And

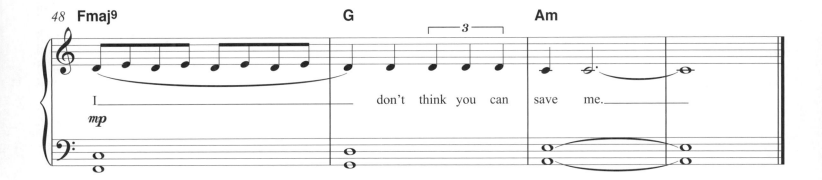

I____ don't think you can save me.

Make You Feel My Love

Words and Music by Bob Dylan

Adele's cover of this Bob Dylan song from his 1997 album, *Time Out of Mind* was the fifth single taken from her debut album *19*, which entered the UK charts at No. 1 on its release in January 2008. Adele's version features in the soundtrack of the 2010 romantic comedy film *When in Rome*.

Hints & Tips: Between bars 17 and 22, take care that the chords sound even; that the notes sound together and not as if they've been spread.

When the rain is blow-ing in your face and the whole world is on your case,

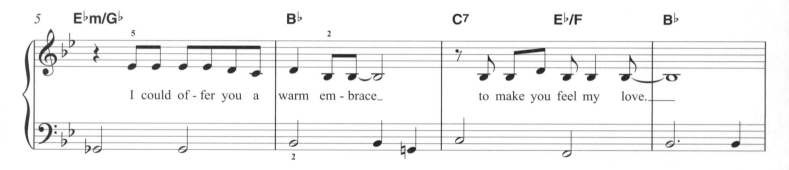

I could of-fer you a warm em-brace to make you feel my love.

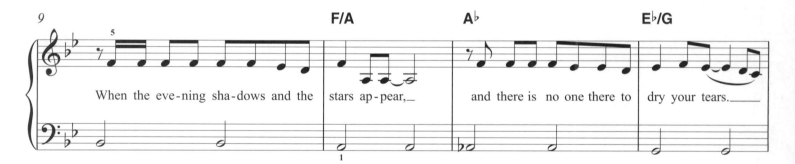

When the eve-ning sha-dows and the stars ap-pear, and there is no one there to dry your tears.

I could hold you for a mil-lion years, to make you feel my love.

Copyright © 1997 UNIVERSAL TUNES
All Rights Reserved   Used by Permission

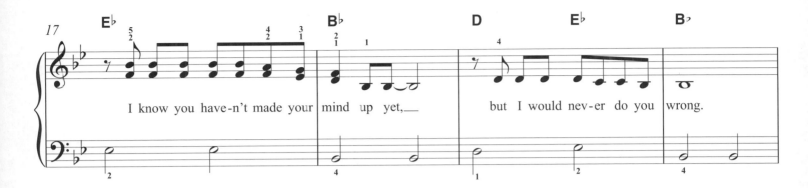

I know you have-n't made your mind up yet,___ but I would nev-er do you wrong.

I've known it from the mo-ment that we___ met,___ no doubt in my mind where you be-

- long.___ I'd go hun-gry, I'd go black and blue.___

I'd go crawl-ing down the av-en-ue.___ No, there's noth-ing that I would-n't do,___

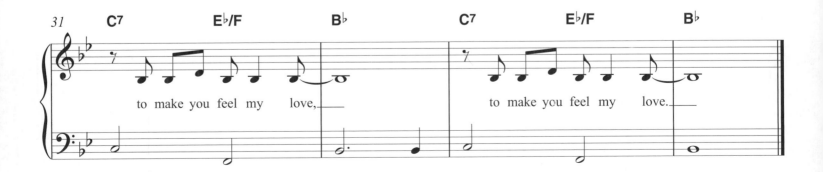

to make you feel my love,___ to make you feel my love.___

Melt My Heart to Stone

Words and Music by Adele Adkins and Francis Eg White

Described by the BBC Sound of 2008 as an "acoustic singer-songwriter who delivers
youthful love songs with a poignant and soulful voice", Adele wrote this track
immediately after breaking up with the boyfriend on whom her debut album is centred.

Hints & Tips: The rhythms in the melody are quite tricky at times, so make
sure you're sure of them before playing through both hands together.

Copyright © 2008 MELTED STONE PUBLISHING LTD. and UNIVERSAL MUSIC PUBLISHING LTD.
All Rights for MELTED STONE PUBLISHING LTD. in the U.S. and Canada Administered by UNIVERSAL - POLYGRAM INTERNATIONAL TUNES, INC.
All Rights for UNIVERSAL MUSIC PUBLISHING LTD. in the U.S. and Canada Administered by UNIVERSAL - POLYGRAM INTERNATIONAL PUBLISHING, INC.
All Rights Reserved   Used by Permission

Million Years Ago

Words and Music by Adele Adkins and Gregory Kurstin

We hear just Adele on vocals and guitar in this track about her yearning to be treated normally, after her shot to fame has affected her personal relationships with loved ones. Longtime friend and collaborator Greg Kurstin wrote this track with Adele, along with two others from the *25* album that 'Million Years Ago' appears on. Kurstin has seen much success as an American producer, having also worked with Sia, Foo Fighters and Paul McCartney, to name a few!

Hints & Tips: This is a gentle number; even when it builds to *forte* in the chorus, it should still sound relaxed. The left hand could be reduced to single notes throughout, especially if the rhythm of the chorus is too tricky.

Copyright © 2015 MELTED STONE PUBLISHING LTD., EMI APRIL MUSIC INC. and KURSTIN MUSIC
All Rights for MELTED STONE PUBLISHING LTD. in the U.S. and Canada Administered by UNIVERSAL - POLYGRAM INTERNATIONAL TUNES, INC.
All Rights for EMI APRIL MUSIC INC. and KURSTIN MUSIC Administered by SONY MUSIC PUBLISHING (US) LLC, 424 Church Street, Suite 1200, Nashville, TN 37219
All Rights Reserved   Used by Permission

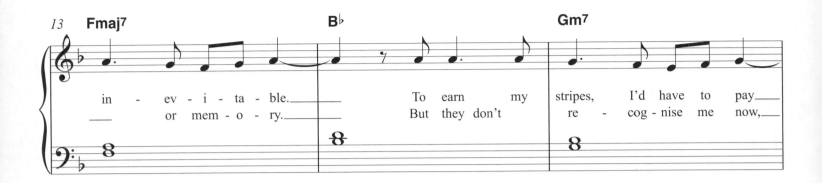

in - ev - i - ta - ble._____
___ or mem - o - ry._____
To earn my stripes, I'd have to pay_____
But they don't re - cog - nise me now,_____

___ and bear my soul.
___ in the light of day.

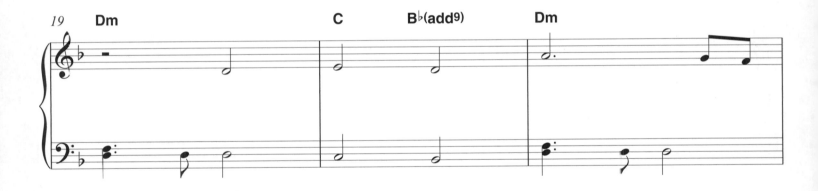

I know I'm

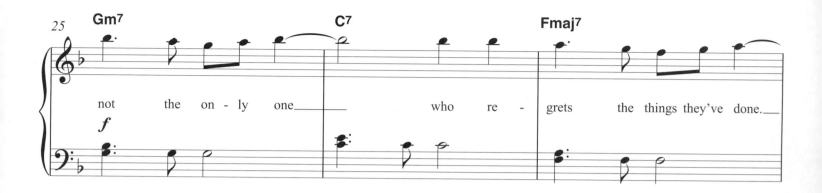

not the on-ly one____ who re - grets the things they've done.____

____ Some-times I just feel it's on-ly me____ who can't stand the re -
who nev-er____ be -

-flec - tion that they see. I wish I could live a lit - tle more,____
-came who they thought they'd be.

____ look up to the sky, not just the floor.____ I feel like my

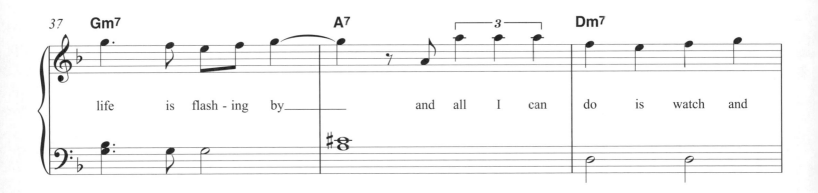

life   is   flash - ing   by____   and all I can   do is watch and

cry.   I   miss   the   air,   I   miss   my   friends,   I   miss   my

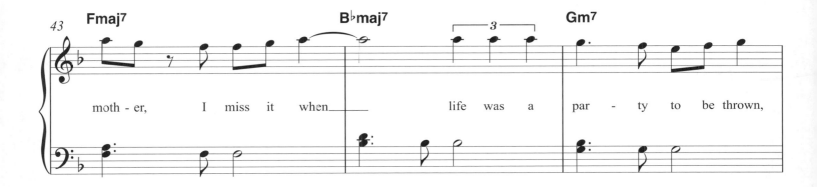

moth - er,   I   miss   it   when____   life   was   a   par - ty   to   be   thrown,

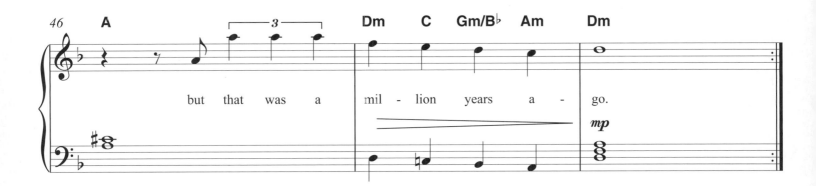

but   that   was   a   mil - lion   years   a - go.

My Little Love

Words and Music by Adele Adkins and Greg Kurstin

This is a particularly intimate and vulnerable track from Adele's 2021 album, *30*, as the listener is let into Adele's inner world via the inclusion of recorded voice notes between herself and her young son in between sung phrases. 'My Little Love' is dedicated to Angelo, her son, while she tries to explain to him about her divorce from his father. Greg Kurstin produced the song in a Golden Age jazz feel, with a prominent string arrangement that runs throughout the piece.

Hints & Tips: Play this song slowly. It needs a calm and relaxed atmosphere, even when it builds up to *forte* in bar 29. Play through the last section as many or few times as you want.

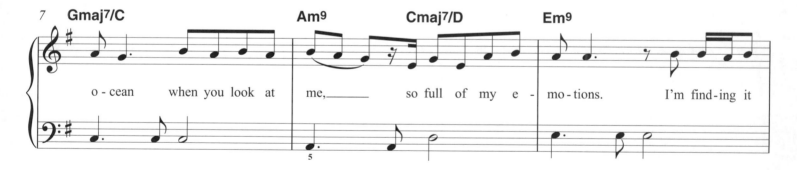

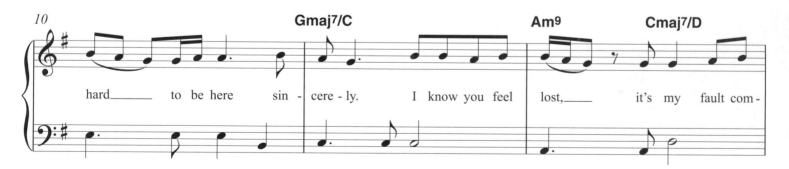

Copyright © 2021 MELTED STONE PUBLISHING LTD., EMI APRIL MUSIC INC. and KURSTIN MUSIC
All Rights for MELTED STONE PUBLISHING LTD. in the U.S. and Canada Administered by UNIVERSAL - POLYGRAM INTERNATIONAL TUNES, INC.
All Rights for EMI APRIL MUSIC INC. and KURSTIN MUSIC Administered by SONY MUSIC PUBLISHING (US) LLC, 424 Church Street, Suite 1200, Nashville, TN 37219
All Rights Reserved   Used by Permission

- plete - ly. (*Spoken:*) *Tell me you love* | *me.* Mmm._____ *I love you*

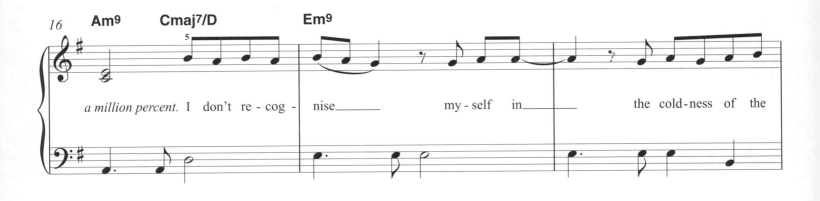

a million percent. I don't re - cog - nise_____ my - self in_____ the cold - ness of the

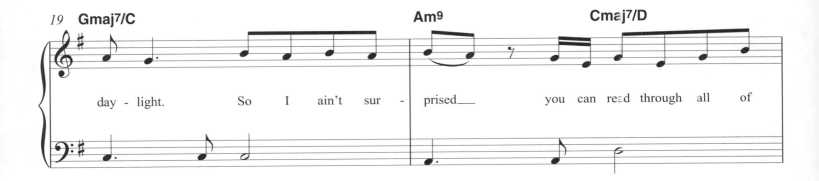

day - light. So I ain't sur - prised_____ you can read through all of

my lies. I feel so bad_____ to be here when I'm so

guil - ty. I'm so far gone____ and you're the on - ly one who can

save me. Mmm.____

I'm hold - in' on, (bare - ly.)____ Ma-ma's got a

lot to learn, (it's hea - vy,)____ I'm hold - in' on,

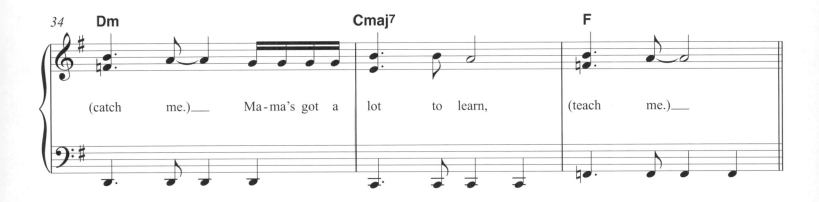

(catch   me.)—   Ma - ma's got a   lot   to   learn,   (teach   me.)—

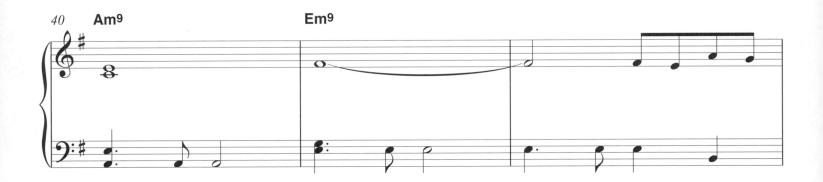

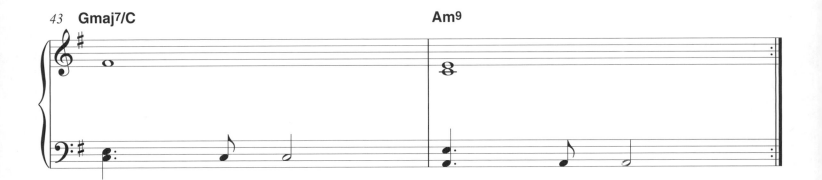

My Same

Words and Music by Adele Adkins

This song charted somewhat unexpectedly in Germany after Lena Meyer-Landrut performed a cover of it on *Unser Star für Oslo*, the TV show through which the German entry to the 2010 *Eurovision Song Contest* was chosen. Lena went on to win the contest and included this song on her debut album.

Hints & Tips: Look out for the accidentals in the left hand; the pattern is quite repetitive, so it should be easy once you've got the hang of it.

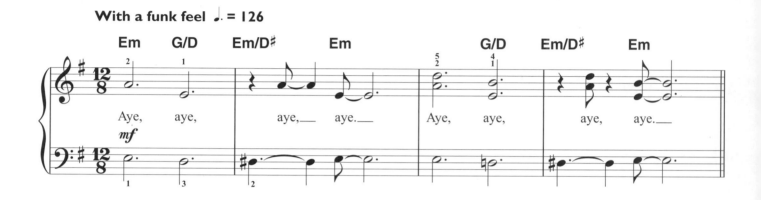

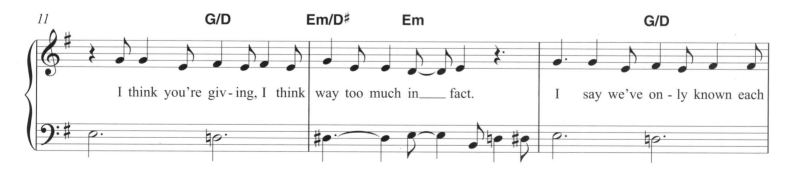

Copyright © 2008 MELTED STONE PUBLISHING LTD.
All Rights in the U.S. and Canada Administered by UNIVERSAL - POLYGRAM INTERNATIONAL TUNES, INC.
All Rights Reserved   Used by Permission

oth - er____ one year.____ You__ say, "Pffft, I've known you long - er,____ my_ dear."

You like to be so close, I like to be a - lone. I like to sit on chairs and

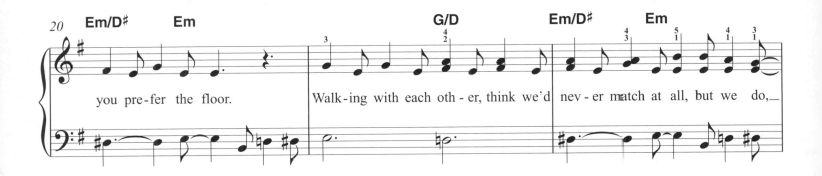

you pre - fer the floor. Walk - ing with each oth - er, think we'd nev - er match at all, but we do,__

__ ooh,__ but we do,__ doo doo doo. But we do,__ ooh,__ but we do,__

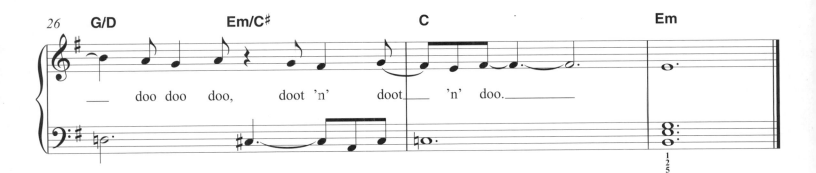

__ doo doo doo, doot 'n' doot__ 'n' doo.____

One and Only

Words and Music by Adele Adkins, Dan Wilson and Greg Wells

Unlike most of the songs on *21*, 'One And Only' is about a male friend whom Adele had known for several years but not dated, despite them being attracted to each other. The middle section was inspired by the description of being kissed by Drew Barrymore's character in the film *Never Been Kissed*.

Hints & Tips: The left hand has mostly steady chords throughout; try to keep them light so they don't overpower the melody.

Copyright © 2010, 2011 MELTED STONE PUBLISHING LTD., BMG MONARCH, SUGAR LAKE MUSIC and FIREHOUSE CAT MUSIC
All Rights for MELTED STONE PUBLISHING LTD. in the U.S. and Canada Administered by UNIVERSAL - POLYGRAM INTERNATIONAL TUNES, INC.
All Rights for BMG MONARCH, SUGAR LAKE MUSIC and FIREHOUSE CAT MUSIC Administered by BMG RIGHTS MANAGEMENT (US) LLC
All Rights Reserved   Used by Permission

why I'm scared, I've been here be - fore. Ev-'ry feel-ing, ev-'ry word, I've i-ma - gined it all.

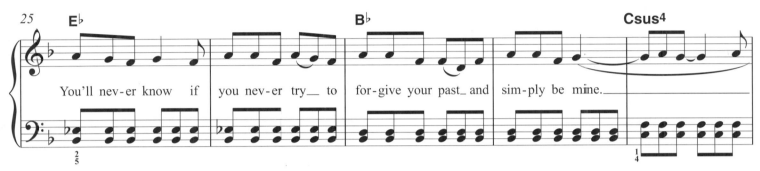

You'll nev-er know if you nev-er try__ to for-give your past_ and sim-ply be mine.__

__ I dare you to__ let me be__ your, your one and on-ly. Prom-ise I'm_

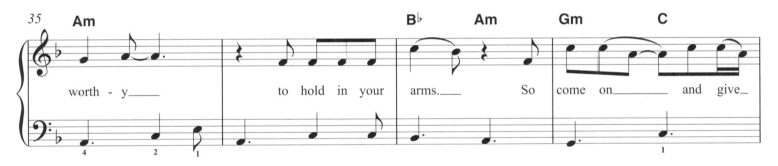

worth - y____ to hold in your arms.__ So come on_____ and give_

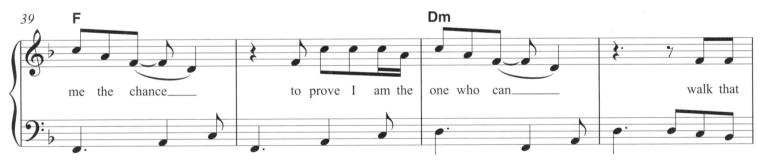

me the chance____ to prove I am the one who can_____ walk that

mile____ un - til the end starts._____

Oh My God

Words and Music by Adele Adkins and Greg Kurstin

Always one to write from personal experience, Adele documents her experience of dating after the breakup of her marriage to Simon Konecki with 'Oh My God'. The song comes from her 2021 album, *30* and is produced by Greg Kurstin. In a slightly new direction for Adele, the track is particularly influenced by R'n'B, with Kurstin recruiting heavyweight drummer Chris Dave, who has played with D'Angelo, Bilal and Anderson .Paak. As for the other instruments on the track, this was all provided by the talented Kurstin himself!

Hints & Tips: The hardest thing with this song is getting the hang of the 'shuffle' rhythm. You will need to spend time playing through the right hand on its own, and listening to the song is a good idea.

Copyright © 2021 MELTED STONE PUBLISHING LTD., EMI APRIL MUSIC INC. and KURSTIN MUSIC
All Rights for MELTED STONE PUBLISHING LTD. in the U.S. and Canada Administered by UNIVERSAL - POLYGRAM INTERNATIONAL TUNES, INC.
All Rights for EMI APRIL MUSIC INC. and KURSTIN MUSIC Administered by SONY MUSIC PUBLISHING (US) LLC, 424 Church Street, Suite 1200, Nashville, TN 37219
All Rights Reserved   Used by Permission

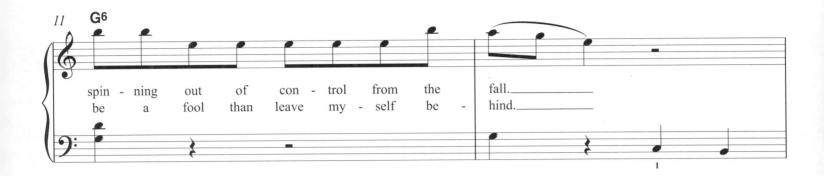

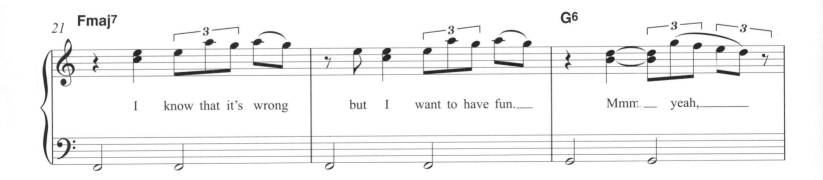

mmm,_____ yeah._____ Oh, my God, I can't be-lieve it, out of

all the peo - ple in the world___ what is the___ like - li - hood of jump-ing

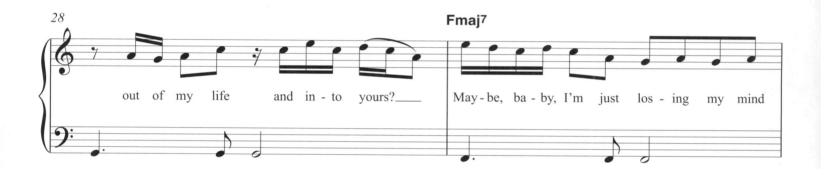

out of my life and in - to yours?___ May-be, ba - by, I'm just los - ing my mind

'cause this is trou - ble but it feels right, tee-t'ring on the edge of Heav - en and Hell,

it's a bat - tle that I can-not fight.___

Remedy

Words and Music by Adele Adkins and Ryan Tedder

This heartrending song was the first written for *25*, composed with the help of past collaborator Ryan Tedder. As soon as she heard his ideas for the song, she knew that it would be about her son, and the track was written and recorded that day. Adele has stated that much of the album is inspired by motherhood, as she had wanted to move away from the younger themes of her previous two albums.

Hints & Tips: Practise the opening semiquavers/sixteenth notes at the start, noting that the thumb shifts down to play the second half of the phrase. Play through this on its own until it feels comfortable.

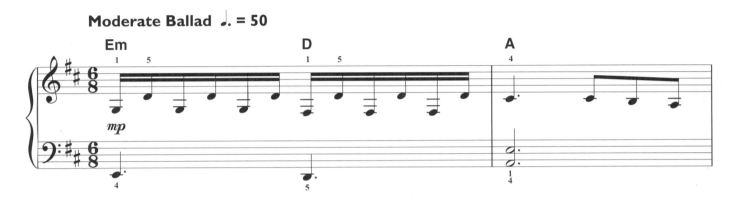

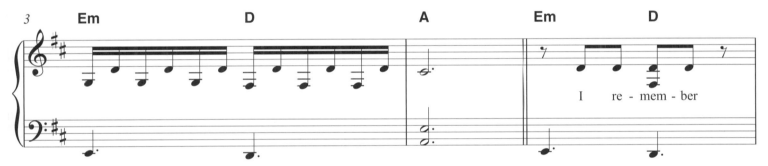

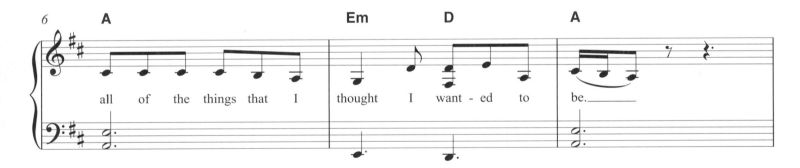

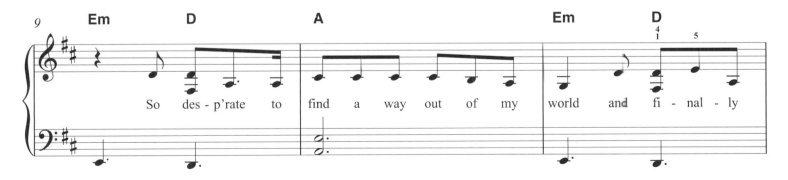

Copyright © 2015 MELTED STONE PUBLISHING LTD. and WRITE ME A SONG PUBLISHING
All Rights for MELTED STONE PUBLISHING LTD. in the U.S. and Canada Administered by UNIVERSAL - POLYGRAM INTERNATIONAL TUNES, INC.
All Rights for WRITE ME A SONG PUBLISHING Administered by DOWNTOWN MUSIC SERVICES
All Rights Reserved   Used by Permission

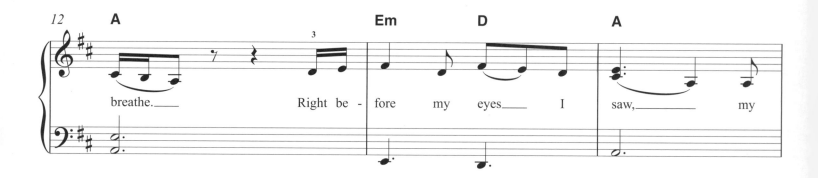

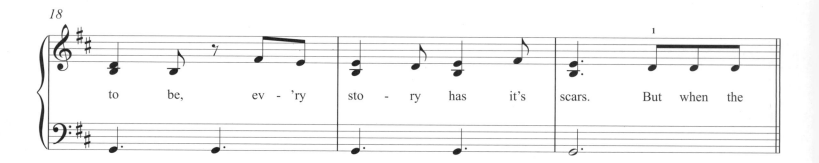

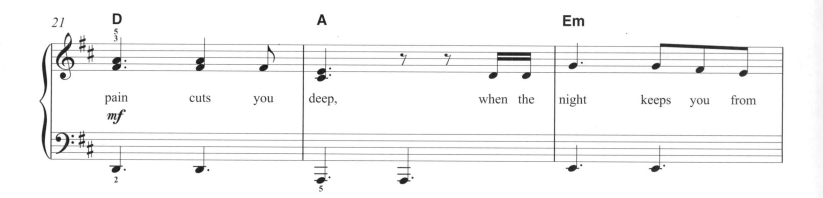

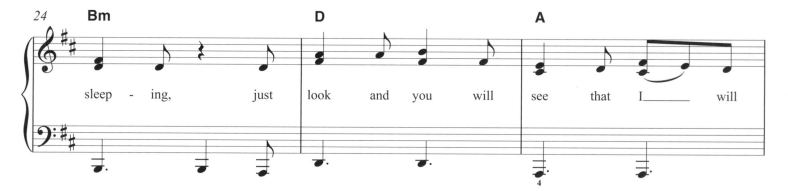

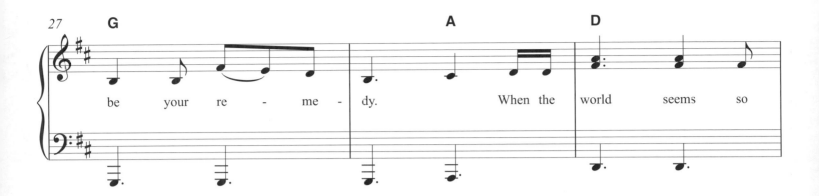

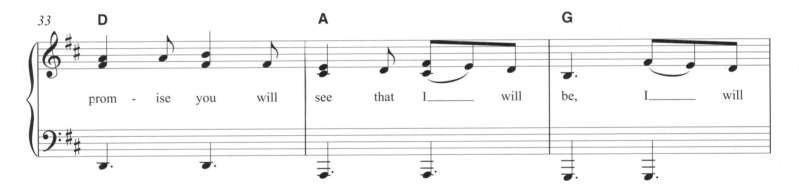

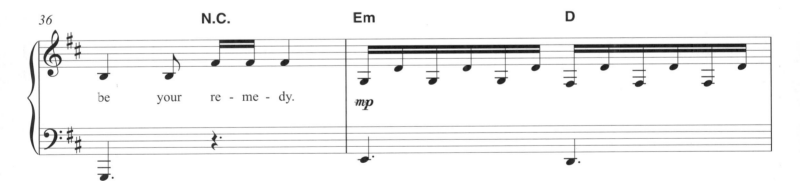

Right as Rain

Words and Music by Adele Adkins, Clay Holley, Jeff Silverman, Nick Movshon and Leon Michels

This song was one of 12 included on Adele's debut album *19*. Released in January 2008, when she was indeed 19 years old, the album debuted at No. 1 in the UK charts in its first week of release. Notably, it also reached No. 2 over three years later as a result of the success of the follow-up album, *21*.

Hints & Tips: This one looks tricky, as there are accidentals in the left hand, but it is a repeated pattern so you should be able to pick it up quite quickly. It's a fast song, so play it through slowly at first and gradually build up the speed.

Who wants to be right as rain? It's bet-ter when some-thing

is wrong. You get ex-cite-ment in your bones and ev-

-er-y-thing you do's a game. When night comes and you're on

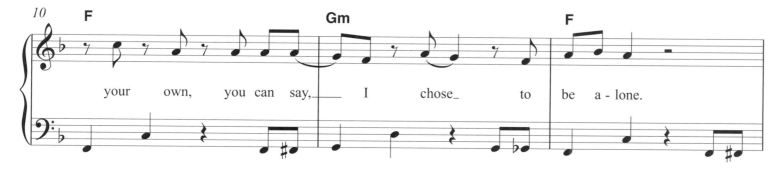

your own, you can say, I chose to be a-lone.

Copyright © 2007, 2008, 2010 MELTED STONE PUBLISHING LTD., SONGS OF THE FOURMULA,
JEFFREY SCOTT PRODUCTIONS, LLC, KOBALT MUSIC SERVICES AMERICA, INC. and BMG PLATINUM SONGS US
All Rights for MELTED STONE PUBLISHING LTD. in the U.S. and Canada Administered by UNIVERSAL - POLYGRAM INTERNATIONAL TUNES, INC.
All Rights for SONGS OF THE FOURMULA Administered by SONY MUSIC PUBLISHING (US) LLC, 424 Church Street, Suite 1200, Nashville, TN 37219
All Rights for JEFFREY SCOTT PRODUCTIONS, LLC and KOBALT MUSIC SERVICES AMERICA, INC. Administered by SONGS OF KOBALT MUSIC PUBLISHING
All Rights for BMG PLATINUM SONGS US Administered by BMG RIGHTS MANAGEMENT (US) LLC
All Rights Reserved   Used by Permission

Who wants to be right as rain? It's hard - er when you're on___

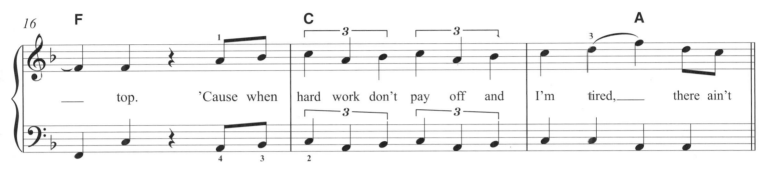

___ top. 'Cause when hard work don't pay off and I'm tired,___ there ain't

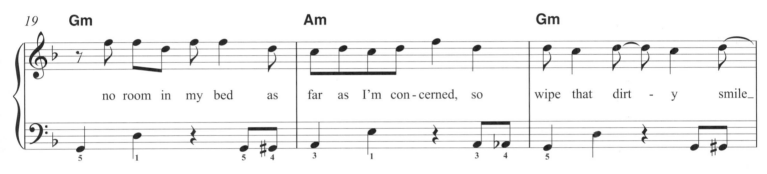

no room in my bed as far as I'm con-cerned, so wipe that dirt - y smile_

___ off. We___ won't be mak-ing up; I've cried my heart out, and

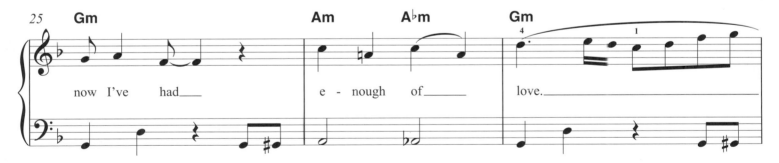

now I've had___ e - nough of___ love.___

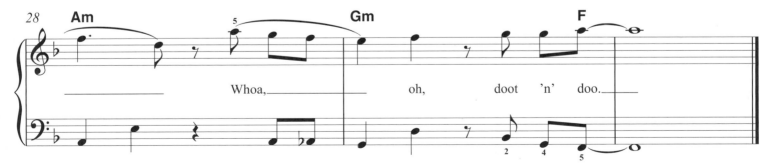

_____ Whoa,___ oh, doot 'n' doo.___

River Lea

Words and Music by Adele Adkins and Brian Burton

The river Adele has named this song after marks the Eastern boundary between her hometown of Tottenham and neighbouring borough, Walthamstow. She sings about being 'stained' by the river and carrying this mark of her upbringing with her, but feeling unable to go back, both spiritually and physically. She has said of the song, "sometimes I get frightened that everyone's going to realise that this [career] is the biggest blag of all time and I'm going to be sent back to Tottenham!". Her hometown is also the focal subject of her debut single, 'Hometown Glory', released in 2007 as part of her debut album, *19*.

Hints & Tips: In this song, the verse feels static, without much pulse. Keep it steady so you can handle the semiquavers/sixteenth notes in the right hand. There is more of a driving rhythm in the chorus, lead by the left hand.

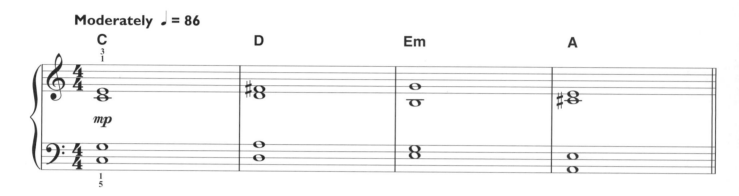

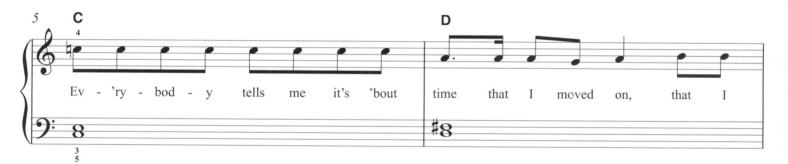

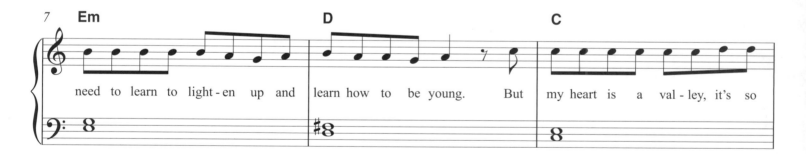

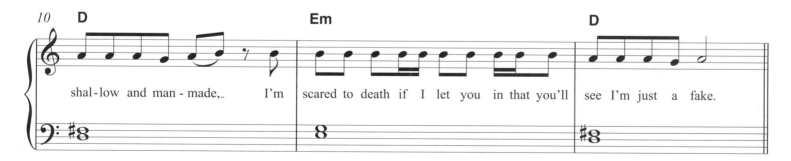

Copyright © 2015 MELTED STONE PUBLISHING LTD. and SWEET SCIENCE
All Rights for MELTED STONE PUBLISHING LTD. in the U.S. and Canada Administered by UNIVERSAL - POLYGRAM INTERNATIONAL TUNES, INC.
All Rights for SWEET SCIENCE Administered Worldwide by KOBALT SONGS MUSIC PUBLISHING
All Rights Reserved   Used by Permission

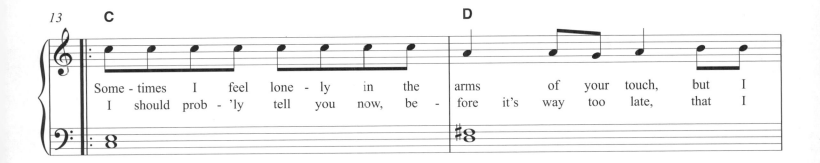

Some - times   I   feel   lone - ly   in   the   arms   of   your   touch,   but   I
I   should   prob - 'ly   tell   you   now,   be -   fore   it's   way   too   late,   that   I

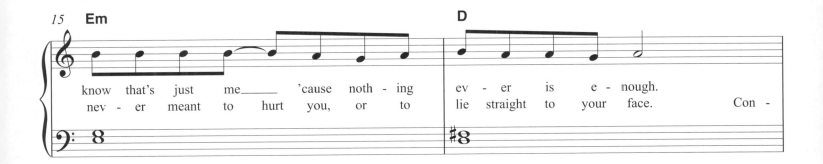

know   that's   just   me_____   'cause   noth - ing   ev - er   is   e - nough.
nev - er   meant   to   hurt   you,   or   to   lie   straight   to   your   face.   Con -

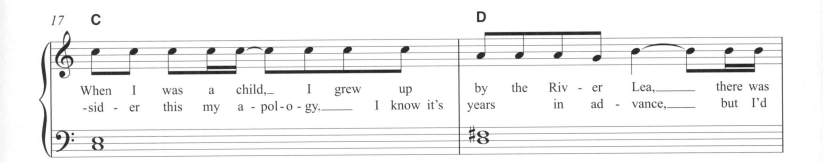

When   I   was   a   child,_   I   grew   up   by   the   Riv - er   Lea,_____   there   was
-sid - er   this   my   a - pol - o - gy._____   I   know   it's   years   in   ad - vance,_____   but   I'd

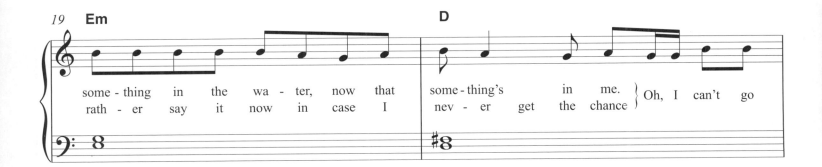

some - thing   in   the   wa - ter,   now   that   some - thing's   in   me. } Oh,   I   can't   go
rath - er   say   it   now   in   case   I   nev - er   get   the   chance

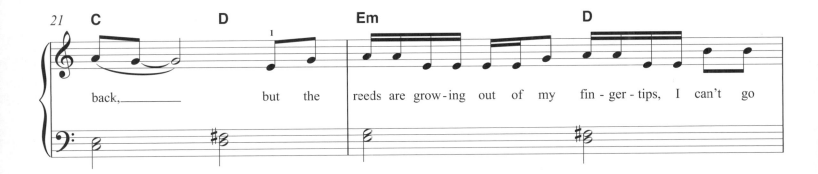

back,_____   but   the   reeds   are   grow - ing   out   of   my   fin - ger - tips,   I   can't   go

79

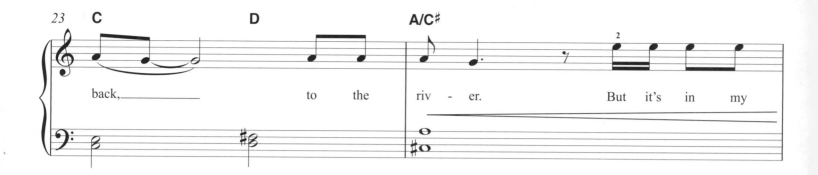

back,_____ to the riv - er. But it's in my

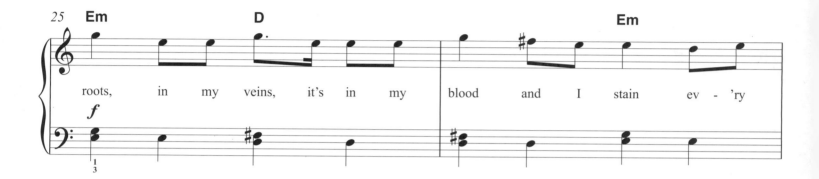

roots, in my veins, it's in my blood and I stain ev - 'ry

heart that I use to heal the pain. Oh, it's in my

roots, in my veins, it's in my blood and I stain ev - 'ry

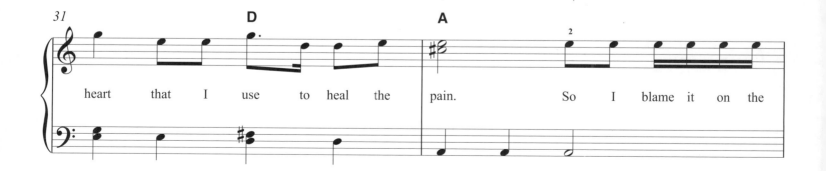

heart that I use to heal the pain. So I blame it on the

Riv - er Lea, ___ the Riv - er Lea, ___ the Riv - er Lea. ___ Yeah, I blame it on the

Riv - er Lea, ___ the Riv - er Lea, ___ the Riv - er Lea. ___

Riv - er Lea, ___ So I blame it on the

Riv - er Lea, ___ the Riv - er Lea, ___ the Riv - er Lea. ___ Yeah, I blame it on the

Riv - er Lea, ___ the Riv - er Lea, ___ the Riv - er Lea. ___

Rolling in the Deep

Words and Music by Adele Adkins and Paul Epworth

The lead single from *21*, this bluesy gospel track reached No. 1 in 11 countries and was her first No. 1
in the US, spending seven weeks at the top of the Billboard Hot 100. The feisty song was Adele's
'heat of the moment' reaction to the argument that marked the end of her relationship.

Hints & Tips: Keep the driving rhythm going in the left hand, making sure it doesn't become disjointed and uneven.

With a driving beat ♩ = 104

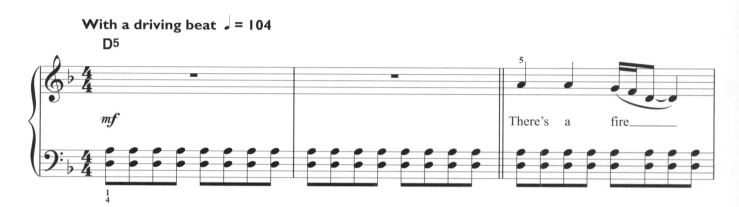

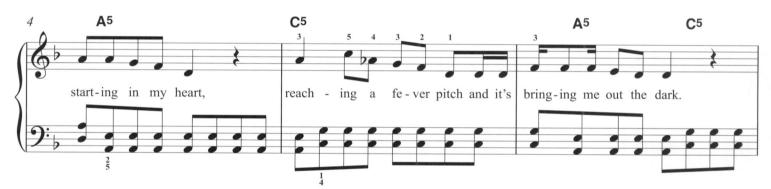

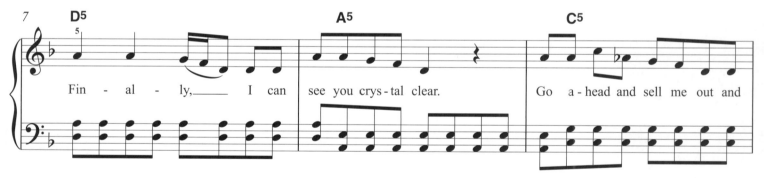

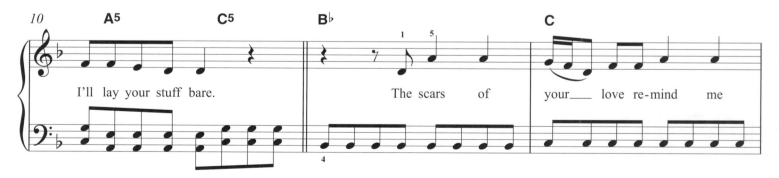

Copyright © 2010, 2011 MELTED STONE PUBLISHING LTD. and EMI MUSIC PUBLISHING LTD.
All Rights for MELTED STONE PUBLISHING LTD. in the U.S. and Canada Administered by UNIVERSAL - POLYGRAM INTERNATIONAL TUNES, INC.
All Rights for EMI MUSIC PUBLISHING LTD. Administered by SONY MUSIC PUBLISHING (US) LLC, 424 Church Street, Suite 1200, Nashville, TN 37219
All Rights Reserved   Used by Permission

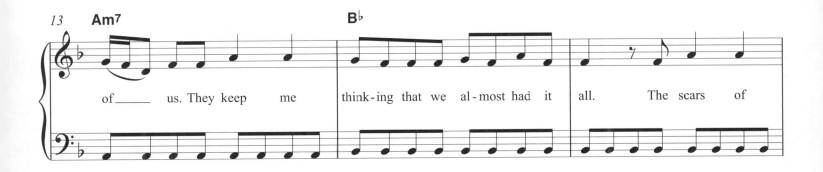

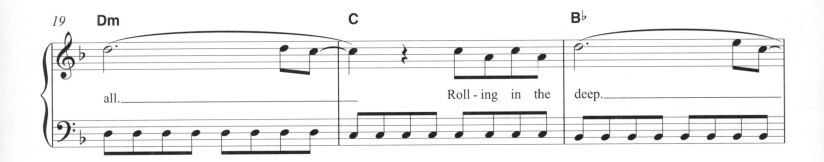

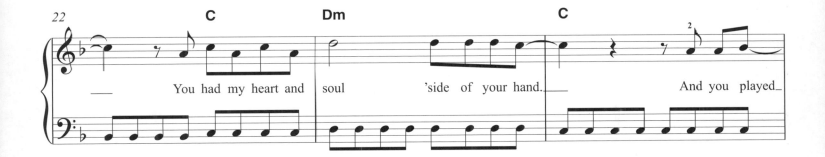

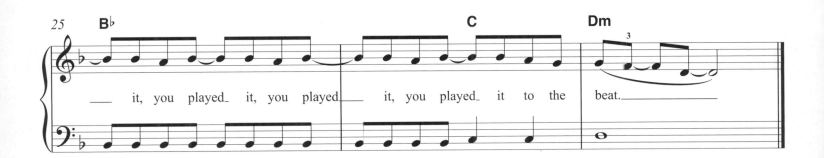

Rumour Has It

Words and Music by Adele Adkins and Ryan Tedder

Despite not being released as a single, this song has appeared on several charts in the US, including the Billboard Hot 100. Rather than being a criticism of the media speculation about her personal life, the song describes the way her own friends gossiped and believed stories about her.

Hints & Tips: The beat should be strong and steady throughout. Where there is nothing going on in the left hand, you'll notice that the drum rhythm has been put in with cross-head notes; you can use this to help you keep time.

With energy and soul ♩ = 120

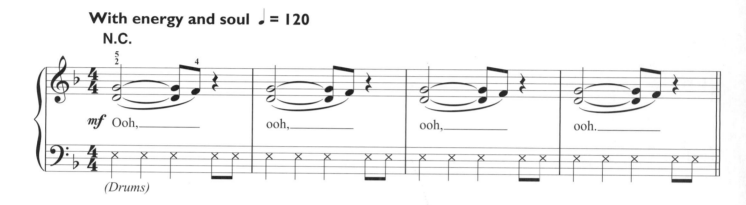

Ooh,_____ ooh,_____ ooh,_____ ooh._____

(Drums)

She, she ain't real.____ She ain't gon' be a-ble to love you like I will.

She is a stran - ger.____ You and I have his-to-ry, or don't you re-mem-ber?

Sure,____ she's got it all. But, ba-by, is that real-ly what you want?____

Copyright © 2011 MELTED STONE PUBLISHING LTD. and WRITE 2 LIVE PUBLISHING
All Rights for MELTED STONE PUBLISHING LTD. in the U.S. and Canada Administered by UNIVERSAL - POLYGRAM INTERNATIONAL TUNES, INC.
All Rights for WRITE 2 LIVE PUBLISHING Administered by DOWNTOWN MUSIC SERVICES
All Rights Reserved   Used by Permission

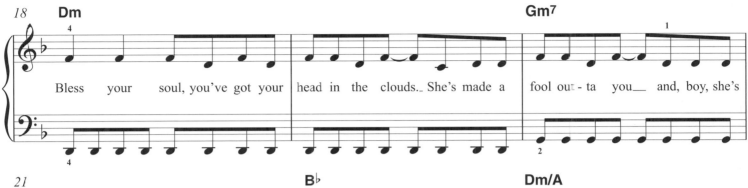

18 Dm

Bless your soul, you've got your head in the clouds._ She's made a fool out-ta you__ and, boy, she's

21 B♭ Dm/A

bring - ing you down._ She made your heart melt, but you're cold to the core._ Now

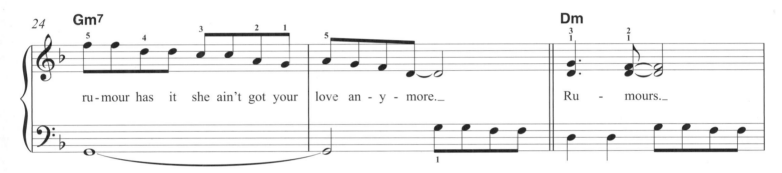

24 Gm7 Dm

ru - mour has it she ain't got your love an - y - more._ Ru - mours._

27

Ru - mours._ Ru - mours._ Ru - mours._

30

Ru - mours._ Ru - mours._ Ru - mours._

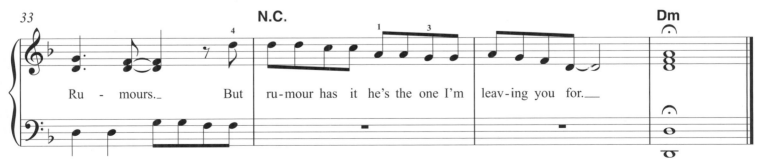

33 N.C. Dm

Ru - mours._ But ru-mour has it he's the one I'm leav-ing you for.__

Send My Love

(To Your New Lover)

Words and Music by Adele Adkins, Max Martin and Shellback

Beginning with a calypso-inspired guitar riff, this song sees Adele address her ex-partner directly,
letting him know that she's over their relationship and completely moved on. The music video
was shot over 12 takes, with various layers of Adele dancing creating a ghostly effect.

Hints & Tips: There are double notes from bar 9 — practise these slowly at first to help you get used to the jumps.

Copyright © 2015 MELTED STONE PUBLISHING LTD., MXM and KMR MUSIC ROYALTIES II SCSP
All Rights for MELTED STONE PUBLISHING LTD. in the U.S. and Canada Administered by UNIVERSAL - POLYGRAM INTERNATIONAL TUNES, INC.
All Rights for MXM and KMR MUSIC ROYALTIES II SCSP Administered Worldwide by KOBALT SONGS MUSIC PUBLISHING
All Rights Reserved   Used by Permission

I'm giv - ing you___ up, I've___ for - gi - en it___ all,

you set me___ free.___

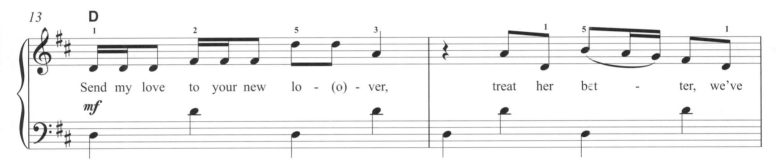

Send my love to your new lo - (o) - ver, treat her bet - ter, we've

got - ta let go of all of our ghosts, we both know we ain't kids no more.___

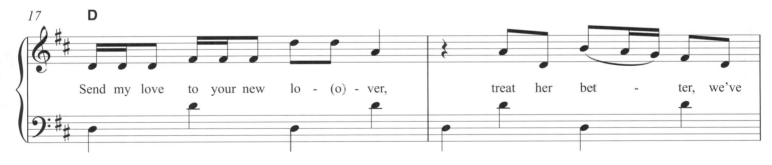

Send my love to your new lo - (o) - ver, treat her bet - ter, we've

got - ta let go of all of our ghosts, we both know we ain't kids no more.___

Set Fire to the Rain

Words and Music by Adele Adkins and Fraser Smith

The third single released from the album *21*, this song, about the contradictions that complicate relationships reached No. 11 in the UK. It was co-written with Fraser T. Smith, one of several songwriters Adele collaborated with for the first time on this album, others being Paul Epworth, Ryan Tedder and Daniel Wilson.

Hints & Tips: Practise the left-hand patterns thoroughly. Go over the right-hand chords in bars 22 and 24, making sure the notes sound together.

Copyright © 2010, 2011 MELTED STONE PUBLISHING LTD. and BMG RIGHTS MANAGEMENT (UK) LTD.
All Rights for MELTED STONE PUBLISHING LTD. in the U.S. and Canada Administered by UNIVERSAL - POLYGRAM INTERNATIONAL TUNES, INC.
All Rights for BMG RIGHTS MANAGEMENT (UK) LTD. Administered by BMG RIGHTS MANAGEMENT (US) LLC
All Rights Reserved   Used by Permission

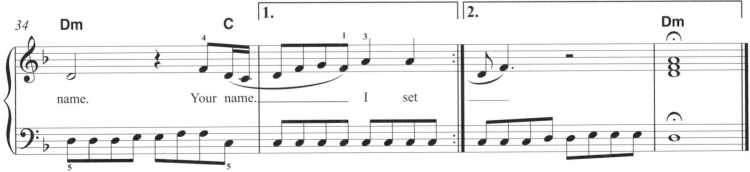

Skyfall

from the Motion Picture SKYFALL

Words and Music by Adele Adkins and Paul Epworth

Skyfall is the third Bond film to star Daniel Craig and the 23rd in the *007* franchise. It is one of only six films to feature the iconic Aston Martin DB5. Sung by Adele, who co-wrote the theme with Paul Epworth, this song is a strong power ballad comparable to the old Bond themes sung by Shirley Bassey.

Hints & Tips: With accidentals cropping up throughout, it may be a good idea to mark in pencil where they occur. Also note where the piece ends after the *D.S.*, with the *Fine* at bar 25.

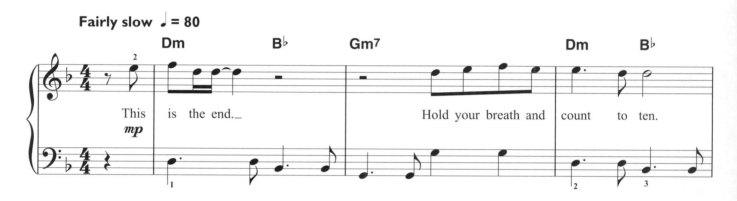

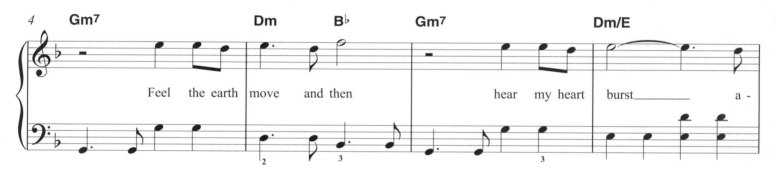

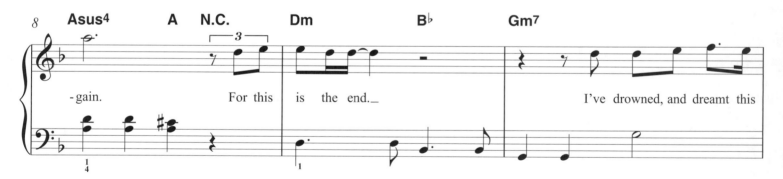

Copyright © 2012 MELTED STONE PUBLISHING LTD. and EMI MUSIC PUBLISHING LTD.
All Rights for MELTED STONE PUBLISHING LTD. in the U.S. and Canada Administered by UNIVERSAL - POLYGRAM INTERNATIONAL TUNES, INC.
All Rights for EMI MUSIC PUBLISHING LTD. Administered by SONY MUSIC PUBLISHING (US) LLC, 424 Church Street, Suite 1200, Nashville, TN 37219
All Rights Reserved   Used by Permission

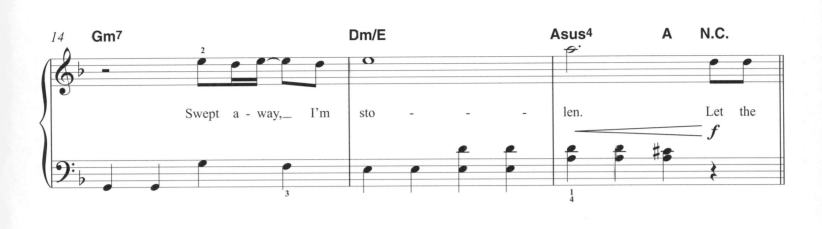

Swept a - way,— I'm sto - - - - len. Let the

sky fall.— When it crum - bles— we will stand tall_____ and face it

all_____ to - geth - er. Let the sky fall.— When it crum - bles— we will

stand tall_____ and face it all to - geth - er, at Sky - fall.

At Sky - fall. Sky - fall is

where we start._ A thou-sand miles and poles a - part._

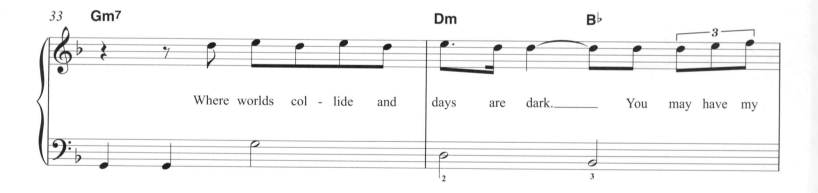

Where worlds col - lide and days are dark._____ You may have my

D.S. al Fine

num - ber, you can take my name but you'll nev - er have my heart. Let the

Someone Like You

Words and Music by Adele Adkins and Dan Wilson

Adele's breathtaking performance of this song at the 2011 BRIT Awards led to it becoming her first
No. 1 single in the UK, a position it held for five weeks. It tells the story of Adele learning of her
ex-boyfriend's engagement and wishing him happiness whilst still longing to find 'someone like him'.

Hints & Tips: Keep the left-hand quavers/eighth notes even and flowing.
Watch out for when the pattern changes in bars 17—20.

Copyright © 2011 MELTED STONE PUBLISHING LTD., BMG MONARCH and SUGAR LAKE MUSIC
All Rights for MELTED STONE PUBLISHING LTD. in the U.S. and Canada Administered by UNIVERSAL - POLYGRAM INTERNATIONAL TUNES, INC.
All Rights for BMG MONARCH and SUGAR LAKE MUSIC Administered by BMG RIGHTS MANAGEMENT (US) LLC
All Rights Reserved   Used by Permission

gave you things_____ I did-n't give to you._____

Old friend, why are you so shy? Ain't like

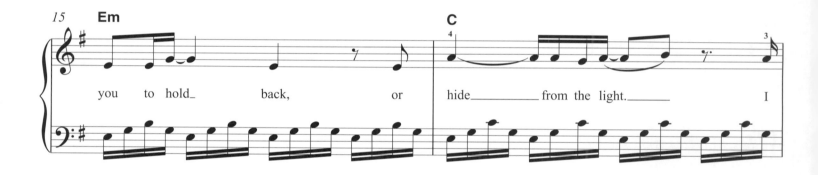

you to hold_ back, or hide_____ from the light._____ I

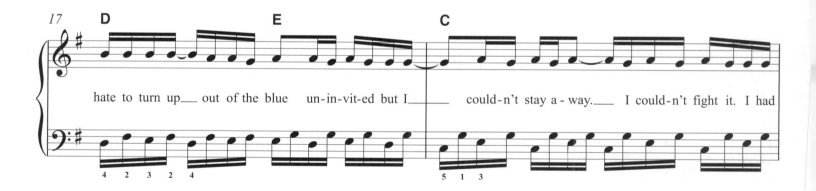

hate to turn up_ out of the blue un-in-vit-ed but I_____ could-n't stay a-way._____ I could-n't fight it. I had

hoped you'd see my face and that you'd be re-mind-ed that for me, it is-n't o - ver._____

Nev-er-mind, I'll find some-one like_ you. I wish

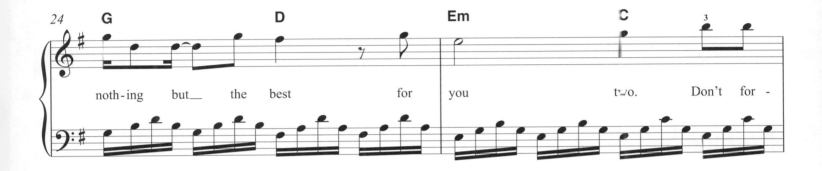

noth-ing but_ the best for you two. Don't for -

-get me, I beg. I'll_ re - mem-ber_____ you said_____ some-times it

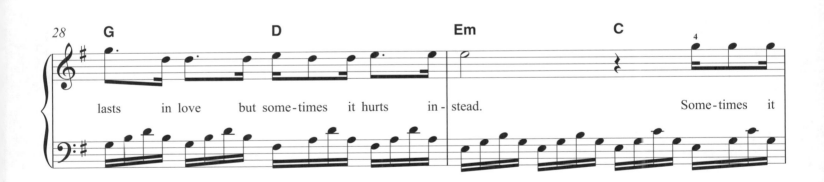

lasts in love but some-times it hurts in - stead. Some-times it

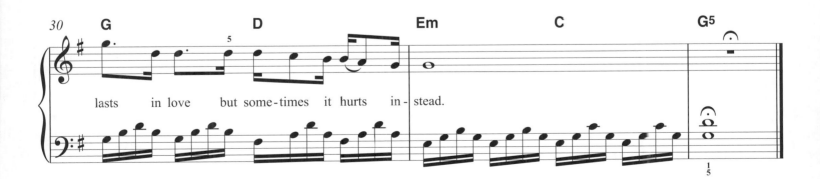

lasts in love but some-times it hurts in - stead.

Take It All

Words and Music by Adele Adkins and Francis Eg White

This soulful ballad explores the early stages of a relationship falling apart. Adele composed the track with Ivor Novello Award-winner Francis "Eg" White, having previously collaborated with him on several tracks from her debut album, including the Grammy Award-winning song 'Chasing Pavements'.

Hints & Tips: As this song is quite slow with chords in the left hand, take care to count out the beats of each bar in your head — or try tapping your foot along — until you've got the hang of the right-hand rhythms.

Copyright © 2011 MELTED STONE PUBLISHING LTD. and UNIVERSAL MUSIC PUBLISHING LTD.
All Rights for MELTED STONE PUBLISHING LTD. in the U.S. and Canada Administered by UNIVERSAL - POLYGRAM INTERNATIONAL TUNES, INC.
All Rights for UNIVERSAL MUSIC PUBLISHING LTD. in the U.S. and Canada Administered by UNIVERSAL - POLYGRAM INTERNATIONAL PUBLISHING, INC.
All Rights Reserved   Used by Permission

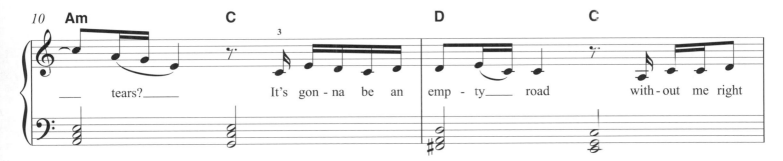

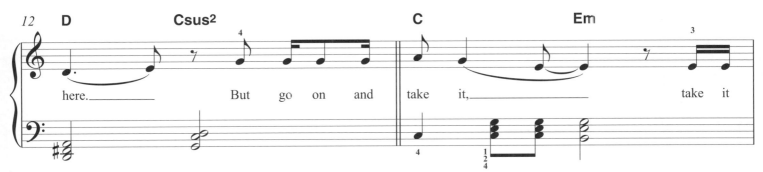

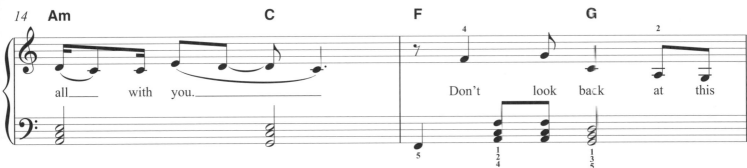

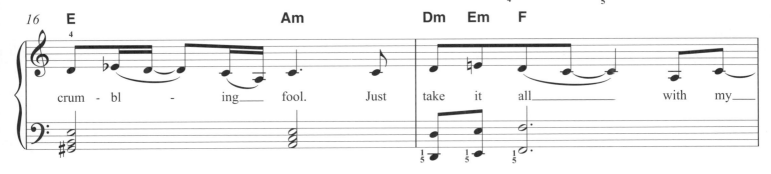

Tired

Words and Music by Adele Adkins and Francis Eg White

Adele's debut album, *19*, from which this track is taken, was nominated for the Nationwide Mercury Prize in 2008 as well as earning Adele Best New Artist at the 2009 Grammy Awards, one of the two awards she claimed from the four nominations she received that year.

Hints & Tips: The left hand should be nice and light; the *staccato* should make it easier to play the left-hand stretches from bar 25.

Synth Pop ♩ = 100

Hold my hand while you cut me down. It had

on - ly just be - gun but now it's o - ver now. And you're

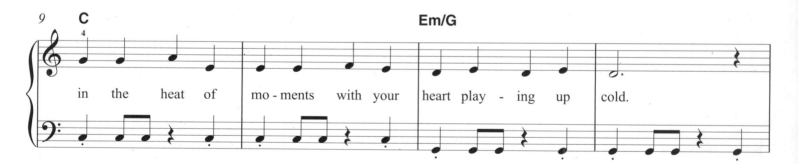

in the heat of mo - ments with your heart play - ing up cold.

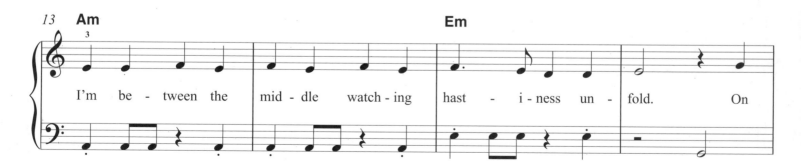

I'm be - tween the mid - dle watch - ing hast - i - ness un - fold. On

Copyright © 2008 MELTED STONE PUBLISHING LTD. and UNIVERSAL MUSIC PUBLISHING LTD.
All Rights for MELTED STONE PUBLISHING LTD. in the U.S. and Canada Administered by UNIVERSAL - POLYGRAM INTERNATIONAL TUNES, INC.
All Rights for UNIVERSAL MUSIC PUBLISHING LTD. in the U.S. and Canada Administered by UNIVERSAL - POLYGRAM INTERNATIONAL PUBLISHING, INC.
All Rights Reserved   Used by Permission

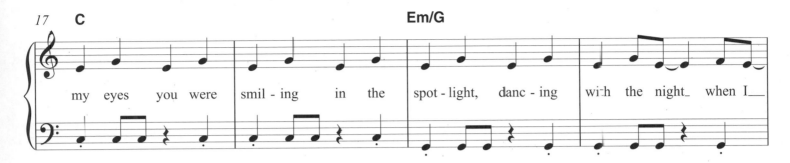

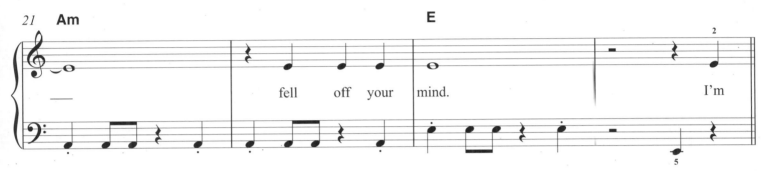

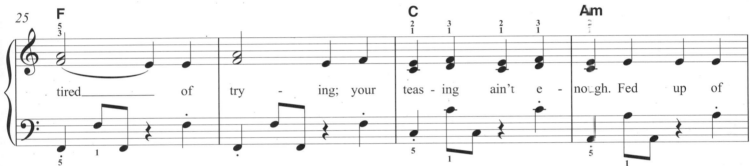

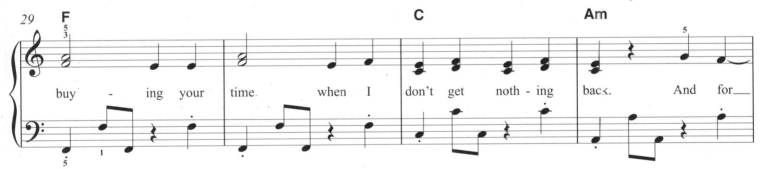

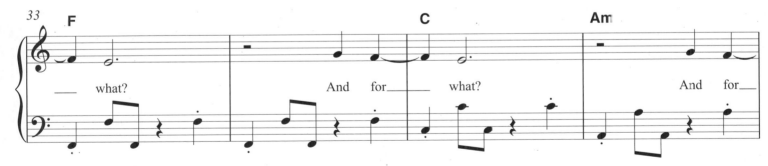

To Be Loved

Words and Music by Adele Adkins and Tobias Jesso Jr.

When her parents split up at the age of two, Adele became estranged from her father, only reconciling shortly before he passed away from cancer in 2021. This piano ballad was written about wanting to have the stable and loving environment that she feels she wasn't able to have from her family upbringing and discovering the parallels that lie between the experience of her parents' divorce and her own. It is a particularly vulnerable song for Adele, who finds it hard to even listen to after recording it for her *30* album.

Hints & Tips: In this song the right hand has a lot more work to do than the left.
It tells the story, while the left hand plays semibreves/whole notes. Keep it steady.

Copyright © 2021 MELTED STONE PUBLISHING LTD. and SONGS OF UNIVERSAL, INC.
All Rights for MELTED STONE PUBLISHING LTD. in the U.S. and Canada Administered by UNIVERSAL - POLYGRAM INTERNATIONAL TUNES, INC.
All Rights Reserved   Used by Permission

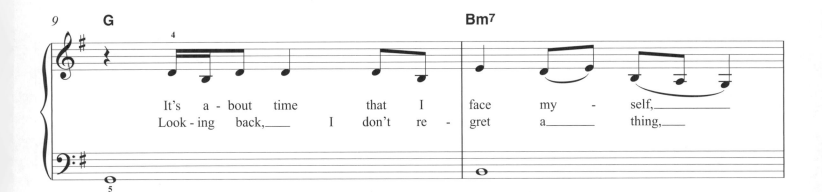

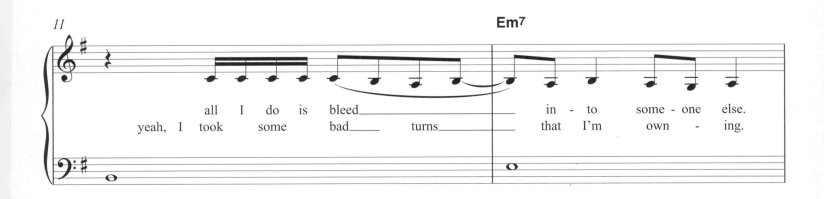

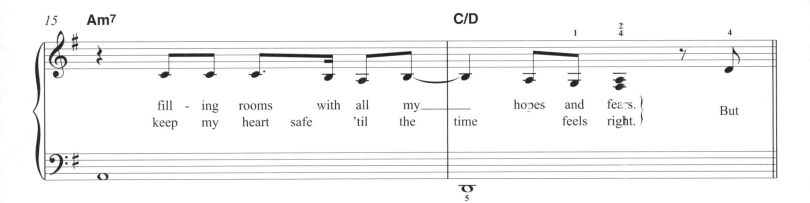

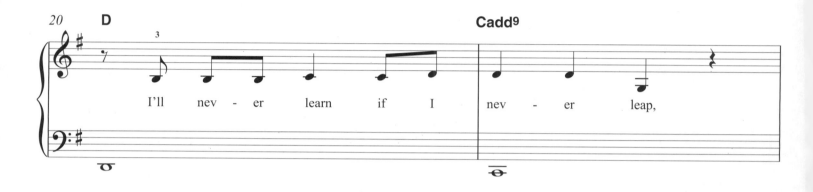

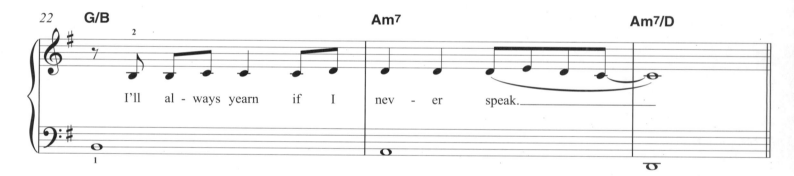

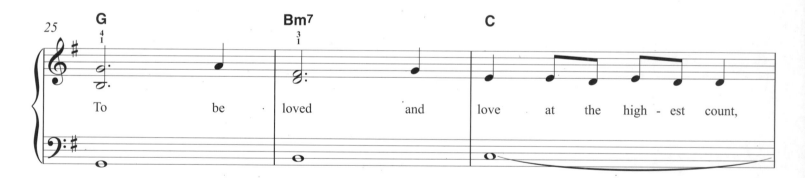

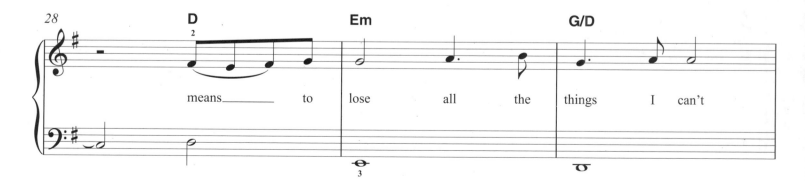

live_____ with-out. Let it be known that I_____ will

choose to lose, it's a sac - ri - fice_____ but I_____

can't live a lie. Let it be known,_____ let it

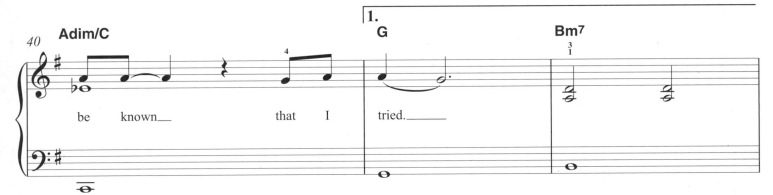

be known_____ that I tried._____

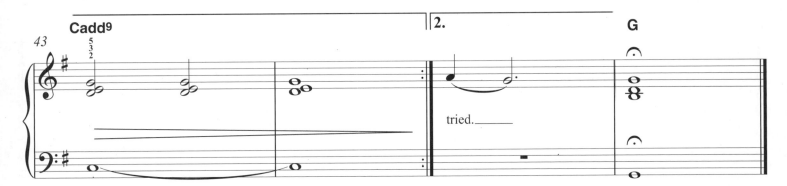

tried._____

Turning Tables

Words and Music by Adele Adkins and Ryan Tedder

This song charted on both the US Billboard Hot 100 and Canadian Hot 100 following a performance
by Gwyneth Paltrow in the role of Holly Holliday on the 20th Century Fox TV show *Glee*.
This was one of two renditions of Adele's songs on the show, the other being 'Rolling in the Deep'.

**Hints & Tips: Keep the left hand loose and flowing and watch out for the stretches.
Practise the tricky rhythm in bars 17—23, noting the change in time signature in bar 22.**

Copyright © 2011 MELTED STONE PUBLISHING LTD. and WRITE 2 LIVE PUBLISHING
All Rights for MELTED STONE PUBLISHING LTD. in the U.S. and Canada Administered by UNIVERSAL - POLYGRAM INTERNATIONAL TUNES, INC.
All Rights for WRITE 2 LIVE PUBLISHING Administered by DOWNTOWN MUSIC SERVICES
All Rights Reserved   Used by Permission

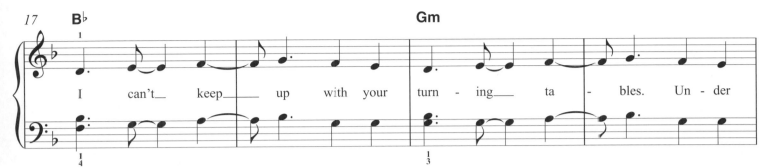

I can't_ keep_ up with your turn - ing_ ta - bles. Un - der

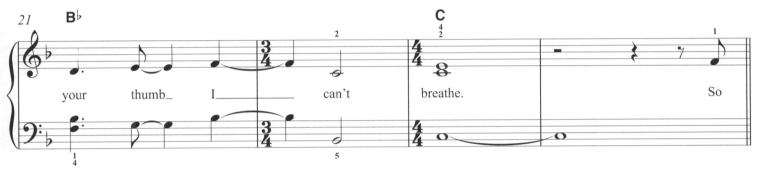

your thumb_ I_ can't breathe. So

I won't let you close e - nough_ to hurt_ me. No,

I won't res - cue you to just_ de - sert_ me. I can't give_

_ you the heart you think_ you gave_ me._ It's time to

say good - bye._ To turn - ing ta - bles._

Water Under the Bridge

Words and Music by Adele Adkins and Gregory Kurstin

Adele teamed up with Greg Kurstin — with whom she wrote 'Hello' and 'Million Years Ago' — to compose this song, dedicated to her partner Simon Konecki. She states that the song is about relationships and how people can work together to overcome any issues, making the relationship stronger as a result.

Hints & Tips: Play through the trickier right-hand rhythms, starting from bar 28, slowly at first, then build up the speed. The steady minims/half notes in the left hand should help you keep time.

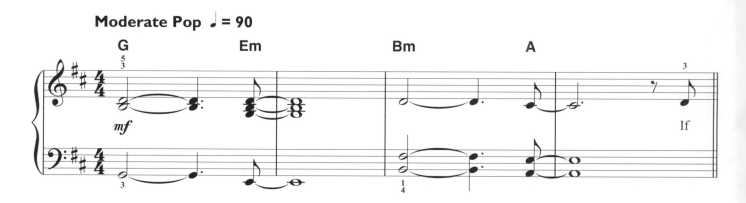

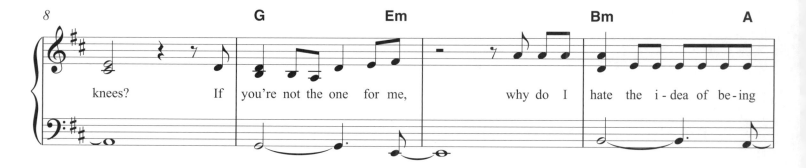

Copyright © 2015 MELTED STONE PUBLISHING LTD., EMI APRIL MUSIC INC. and KURSTIN MUSIC
All Rights for MELTED STONE PUBLISHING LTD. in the U.S. and Canada Administered by UNIVERSAL - POLYGRAM INTERNATIONAL TUNES, INC.
All Rights for EMI APRIL MUSIC INC. and KURSTIN MUSIC Administered by SONY MUSIC PUBLISHING (US) LLC, 424 Church Street, Suite 1200, Nashville, TN 37219
All Rights Reserved   Used by Permission

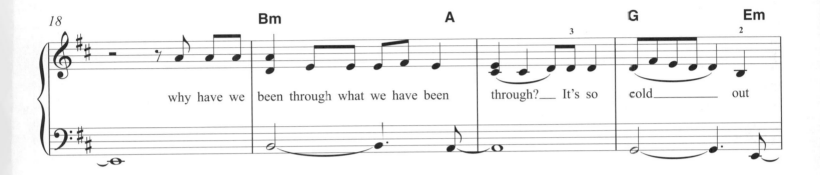

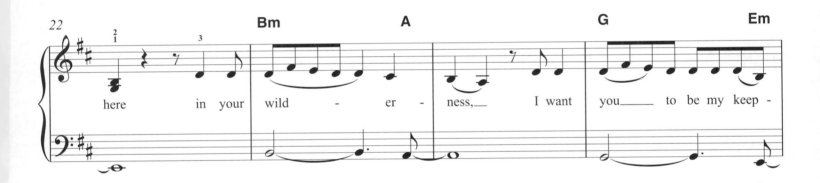

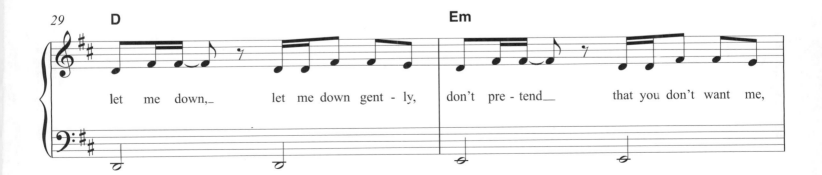

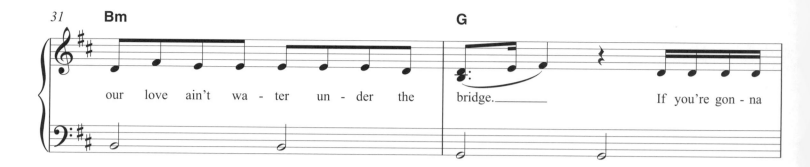

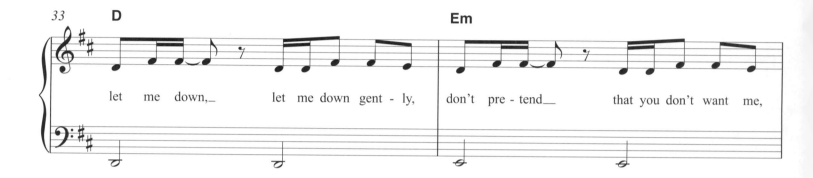

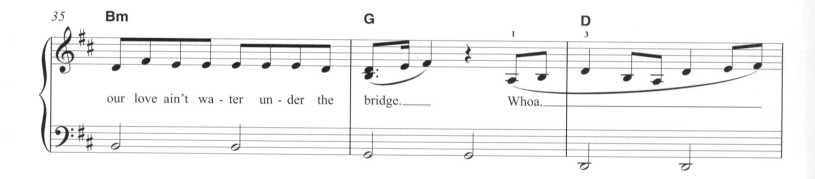

When We Were Young

Words and Music by Adele Adkins and Tobias Jesso Jr.

This song was reportedly composed by Adele and Tobias Jesso Jr. on a piano that used to belong to composer Philip Glass. Adele has stated that of all the songs on *25*, this one means the most to her because it's about spending time with old friends, reminiscing, and "feeling like you're 15 again".

Hints & Tips: The right hand goes quite low in this. Write out any of the notes you're unsure of in pencil, then you can erase them when you're confident!

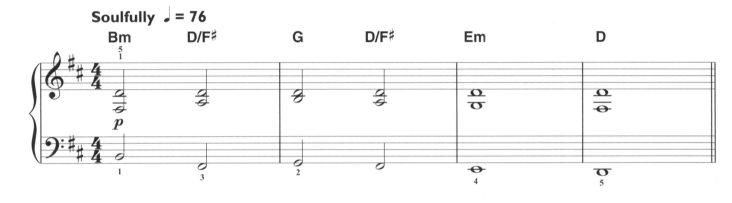

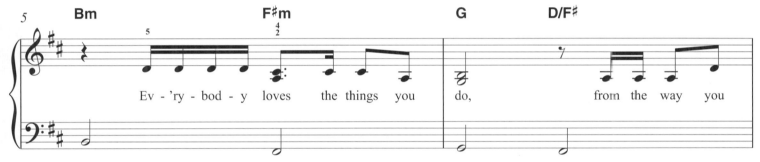

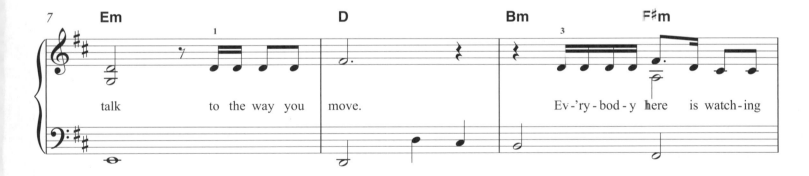

Copyright © 2015 MELTED STONE PUBLISHING LTD. and SONGS OF UNIVERSAL, INC.
All Rights for MELTED STONE PUBLISHING LTD. in the U.S. and Canada Administered by UNIVERSAL - POLYGRAM INTERNATIONAL TUNES, INC.
All Rights Reserved   Used by Permission

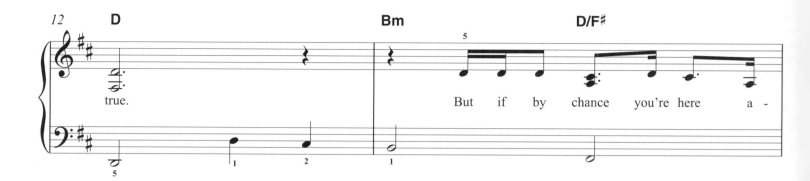

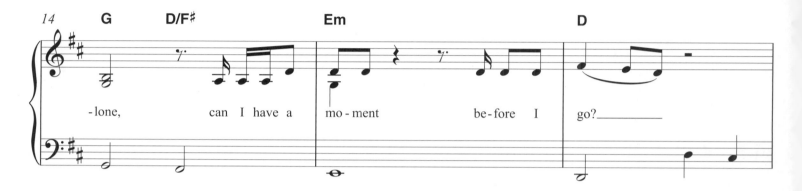

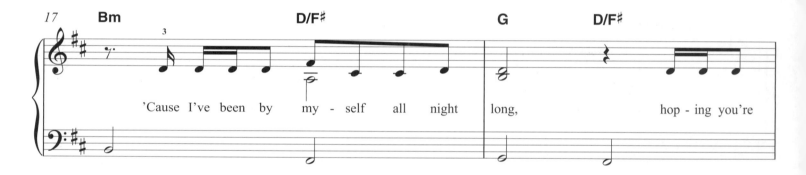

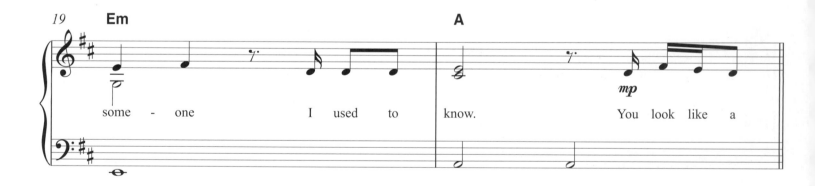

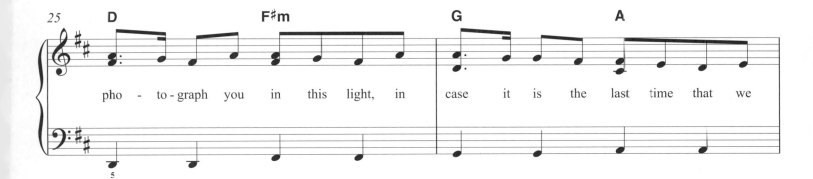

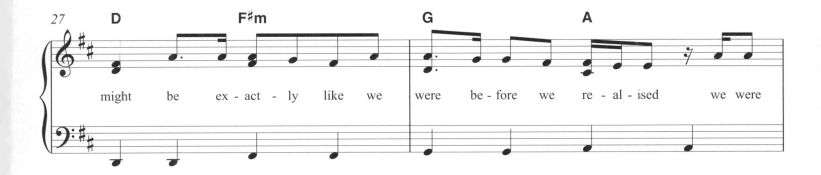

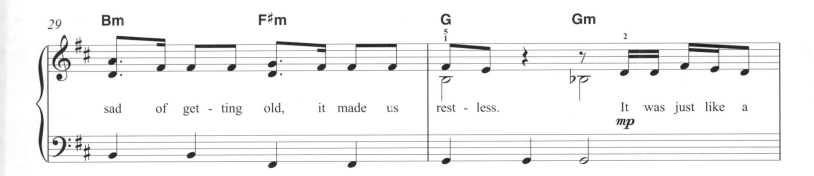

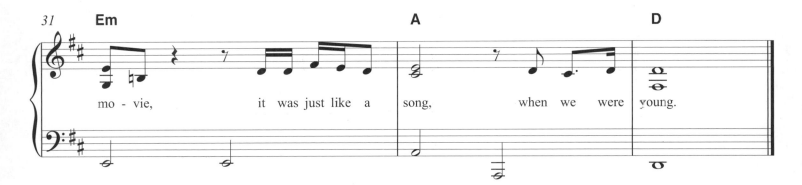